"*Psalms of COVID-19* i.
cal philosophy of life with remarkable success. The book is about the virtue of gratitude, which is drowned in the current global culture of materialism, individualism, utilitarianism, and hedonism. A constant disposition of gratitude for our being and becoming would make our life more authentic, meaningful, and worth living. A contemplative and introspective reading of this inspiring book will be highly beneficial to the reader."

—JOSEPH ETHAKUZHY
Professor of Philosophy, St. Peter's Pontifical
Institute, Bangalore, India

"When we go through the pages of *Psalms of COVID-19*, we are filled with a sense of gratitude for all that we have received from God, nature, and others; we begin to appreciate rather than complain; we resort to cherishing rather than discarding; we begin to protect what we have been given rather than exploit; and ultimately, we become more generous rather than selfish."

—THOMAS THARAYIL
Auxiliary Bishop of Changanacherry

"I congratulate Matthew Palai for this remarkable work, which is beautifully drafted in the model of the Psalms. The reflections therein suit very much the contemporary situation beset with the pandemic of COVID-19 . . . These lines soothe the psyche with a healing touch and take the readers to the divine power."

—KURIAKOSE BHARANIKULANGARA
Archbishop of Faridabad-Delhi

"I consider this book a meaningful meditation for our present-day lifestyle. All the social evils present in modern affluent societies are very beautifully candy-wrapped in the form of prayers embedded throughout the book. This book is the fruit of deep contemplation based on observation, vision, and values, with support from science, philosophy, and theology."

—**RAPHAEL THATTIL**
Bishop of Shamshabad (Hyderabad)

Psalms of COVID-19

Psalms of COVID-19

Matthew Palai

Foreword by Mar Raphael Thattil

RESOURCE *Publications* · Eugene, Oregon

PSALMS OF COVID-19

Resource Publications
An Imprint of Wipf and Stock Publishers
199 W. 8th Ave., Suite 3
Eugene, OR 97401

www.wipfandstock.com

PAPERBACK ISBN: 978-1-6667-3127-9
HARDCOVER ISBN: 978-1-6667-2360-1
EBOOK ISBN: 978-1-6667-2361-8

11/16/21

Contents

Foreword by Mar Raphael Thattil | vii

Preface | xi

Introduction | xv

Part I | 1

1 Parents: The Ambassadors of God on Earth | 3

2 The Traditional Family: The Heaven on Earth | 9

3 Born Healthy: The Greatest Boon | 16

4 Time: The Nonexistent Existent | 21

5 The Eyes: The Most Delightful Sense | 28

6 Speech and Hearing: The Bridge to People | 34

7 Taste: The Most Enjoyed Sense | 39

8 The Sense of Smell: The Chimney of Relations | 44

9 Talents: The Special Gifts from God | 49

10 Inventions and Discoveries: The Mother of Necessities | 54

11 The Unique Self: The Image and Likeness of God | 60

Part II | 67

12 The Earth: The Pond of the Science-Frog | 69

13 The Precious Water: The Universal Solvent | 75

14 The Sun: The Propellor of Life on Earth | 80

15 The Wind: The Sun's Winnow | 85

16 The Atmosphere: The Fortification of Earth | 89

17   Photosynthesis: The Scaffold of Life | 93

18   Oxygen: The Soul of Life | 97

19   The Staple Foods: The Fuel of the Body | 102

20   The Produce: The Universal Food | 107

21   Animals: The *Sine Qua Nons* | 113

22   The Ancillary Helpers: The Stagehands | 118

23   Trees: The Silent Benefactors | 125

24   The Mountains: The Top of the World | 129

Part III | 133

25   Creation and Sustenance: Ex Nihilo Nihil Fit | 135

26   Motion and Sustenance: The Unmoved Mover | 140

Part IV | 145

27   The Cross of Christ: Attunement of Human Will | 147

28   God: The Omnipresent Benefactor | 166

Endorsements | 169

Bibliography | 173

Foreword

It gives me immense pleasure to write the foreword to the new book *Psalms of COVID-19,* written by Matthew Palai, a friend of mine in the United States of America. The term "Psalms" naturally recalls the book of Psalms of the Old Testament, which is a poetic expression of the innermost thoughts, feelings, frustrations, and questions of men who were close to God. The author, with an eye of a prophet, views and assesses the lifestyles of the present generation and modern society, which are affected by the virus of egoism, hedonism, and materialism. The book can be summed up as a wake-up call to the modern society like the wake-up call of the prophet Nathan to King David. The author clearly states that "it is time to repent and return to the Almighty." The objectivity of the arguments makes the book applicable to the whole world, irrespective of locality or religion.

When I was requested to write a foreword for this book, I accepted it wholeheartedly as I knew that it would be another gem from the bottom of the Mariana Trench. I had read a previous book written by the author, *The Lord's Prayer: Live It or Quit Saying It*, and was much impressed by the author's interpretation and vision of the meaning of the Lord's Prayer which changed even my own ways of saying the Lord's Prayer. Reading this book convinced me that Matthew Palai's books are of a different genre.

If you permit me to compare this book to a garment, the theme of gratitude is the thread by which the whole garment is woven. The quality and authenticity of a person arises from the attitude of gratitude.

The author divides the book into four parts. The first part is based on the theme of "Our being in the image and likeness of God." Procreation is the continuation of God's creation, and our family and parents are instruments in the hands of God. The eleven psalms in the first part of the book help the reader to look back with a heart filled with gratitude to all who have contributed to our being and becoming.

The second part of the book is a meditation of being grateful for the rich variety of nature—the earth, water, sun, wind, atmosphere, oxygen, trees, animals, mountains, etc. As they are given to us *gratis* we take them for granted, feeling neither obligation nor gratitude. It is the exploitation of nature that makes our life on earth miserable. The second part of the book convinces us that we can see God in anything and everything in our daily life.

The third part of this book poses a challenge to human society to be responsible for the sustenance of nature and the world. As nature takes extra caution for our safety and health, we too must be responsible for the well-being of nature and our surroundings. Man shall not only be a consumer but also a custodian of nature. Ecology is not mere knowledge found in books; rather, it should be a spirituality of our lifestyle. With simple analogies, the author establishes that the universe is not the result of an unplanned chaotic bang, but the outcome of ingenious design.

The last part of this book is about Jesus our Redeemer and the Omnipresent Benefactor, God. Jesus shall become a source of inspiration and imitation. He redeemed the whole world by his suffering and death. The author stresses the importance of accepting and carrying the crosses of our daily life to be true followers of Christ. The book motivates the reader to continue the redemption of Jesus by fulfilling our responsibility towards ourselves, our neighbors, and nature. The last part opens the reader's eyes to see God in anything and everything around us.

I consider this book a meaningful meditation for our present-day lifestyle. All the social evils present in modern, affluent societies are very beautifully candy-wrapped in the form of prayers embedded throughout the book. This book is the fruit of deep contemplation based on observation, vision, and values, with support rooted throughout from science, philosophy, and theology. I place on record my sincere appreciation to the author for the brain and pain he has invested in writing this book. *Psalms of Covid-19* will be a beautiful gift to readers to make life more beautiful.

Mar Dr. Raphael Thattil
Bishop of Shamshabad
(Hyderabad)Date: 22–6-2021

Preface

THIS BOOK IS INTENDED for every living soul on earth who, knowingly or unknowingly, has been enjoying many gifts and favors of others during this wonderful life on earth. This book opens the door for a reflection of our life by trying to open our purblind eyes, which are unable to see the countless blessings that we have been receiving from heaven and earth, and to ponder our attitude towards all the gifts and favors that were showered upon us by the benevolence of other human beings and the Almighty. If no gratitude was shown to those entities, then the pretension of showing gratitude to an unseen Almighty is ostentatious. The goal of this book is to help the reader realize that we can find God in anything and everything around us. We are a product of the benevolence and beneficence of others. Even our subsistence in existence is at the mercy of many seen and unseen benefactors on earth and in heaven, and not acknowledging this is a self-defeating act.

The inspiration for this book comes from the author's observation of the appalling mindset of ingratitude, or taking things for granted, a relational disposability of persons and relationships that is comparable to the disposal of worn-out furniture, the degradation of human relations into consumption goods, the flourishing of hedonistic utilitarianism at individual, social, and global levels, and the entitled attitude of a generation which is at the apex of egocentric self-absorption, embracing materialism and hedonism. It is time to repent and return to the Almighty, as in the parable of the prodigal son. The book is written in an occidental, Christian perspective, but it is applicable to the whole world irrespective of locality or religion, as gratitude has no locality or religion.

Many consider themselves as the masters of the universe they live in, as if everyone else or everything else is under them and was created for their use and happiness, forgetting the naked truth that their life is as evanescent and ephemeral as that of the bubbles that form in a flowing stream. All human relationships have caved in to a benefit—self consumerism. The COVID-19 pandemic has taught us that we are not the masters of the universe and nothing is in our control, in contrast to our belief that everything is under our control. When people are succumbing to COVID-19 in solitude at home, and in hospital beds, save for their guardian angels, it is a good time to think about how we came to be in existence, what we brought with us when we were born into the world, how we have reached where we are now, how much of the facilities we use now actually belong to us, what have we given in return for all the benefits we have received from heaven and earth, and how much of what we have now we are going to pack up with us to the next world.

It is also a good time to think why affluent countries were hit hard by the COVID-19 pandemic. Google and take a close look at the chart, *COVID-19 Map-John Hopkins Coronavirus Resource Center-Critical Trends-mortality analyses-cases and mortality by country.*[1] Look at the death/100,000. As of mid-March 2021, excluding few outliers/loners, the richest and the most technologically advanced countries in the world, such as San Marino, the United Kingdom, Luxembourg, Italy, Portugal, the United States of America, Sweden, Switzerland, Ireland, etc. reeled under the vicious attack of the Coronavirus with a higher death rate per 100,000, whereas the poorest countries, such as Burundi, Tanzania, Central African Republic, Mozambique, Haiti, Uganda, Nigeria, Zambia, etc. had the lowest death rates. In general, the death rate per 100,000 is remarkably high in affluent countries and

1. https://coronavirus.jhu.edu/data/mortality.

comparatively low in poor countries, except for a few outliers. This should have been, normally, the other way around. Even though diseases and death do not differentiate between the rich and the poor, that does not seem to be the case with COVID-19. It may be either that the affluent countries are the Sodom and Gomorrah mentioned in the book of Genesis, or that they are the real living Jobs being tested by God for their fidelity, as in the didactic story of Job, or perhaps there are other compelling reasons for such unexpected death rates which are inversely proportional to the quality-of-life index.

We are living in a world dominated by individualism, narcissism, bureaucracy, and kratocracy. Most religions have caved in the face of rituality and utilitarianism. The needs of self-actualization, culminating in transcendence in Maslow's hierarchy of needs, have disappeared from the hierarchy of the needs of the current world. The *esteem* needs only make sense if they are related to vain prestige. It is time to take a U-turn and to show some gratitude to all entities who have contributed to our well-being. It is also time to thank the unseen Power who has provided us with most of the things that we use and enjoy in this life, whether knowingly or unknowingly.

This is not a book on science, but a book on the basic virtue of gratitude. Most of the content given in this book is based on observation, life experience, and general knowledge. The generalizations, inferences, and ballpark estimates given in this book are based on the author's experience and observation of the world, and are not tied to any specific scientific data or statistics. References to the cosmos, nature, and the modus operandi of various animate and inanimate beings/forces/phenomena present around us are discussed not to explain the science behind them, but to show how they are contributing to our existence and well-being, and how we are benefitting from them. So, this book is not to be treated as a book on *how things work*, but rather, it is to show how unaware we are of the benefits of nature, the ecosystems, and the society around us, all of which are taken for granted by many.

This is not a book on philosophy or theology either. References to some philosophical and theological concepts are made, in as much as they are relevant to the subject of *gratitude,* and as such this book is not to be treated as a book on those lofty subjects. Some content is allegorical, and the readers may have to use their imagination to understand the underlying secondary meaning. They are there to help the readers to see beyond science and materialism, as the latter has a negative effect on the ultimate outcome and satisfaction in life.

Criticizing any individual, group, society, or social practices is not the intent of this book, but they are there to show how these entities/practices are in juxtaposition to the virtue of gratitude. The first chapter of the book is a bird's-eye view of *gratitude* according to various philosophers, theologians, and sages. The ideas mentioned in this book are solely the opinion of the author. They do not represent the doctrines or teachings of any group, religion, or religious organization, and as such the readers may use their discretion in using this book. Contemplative and introspective reading is recommended for this book.

Introduction
Gratitude: *Virtue, Duty, Justice*

THE WORD GRATITUDE COMES from the Latin word *gratus,* which means "pleasing" or "thankful." It is a virtue on account of which a person acknowledges the gift received from another and is thankful to the person who gave the gift, verbally expresses the thankfulness, and makes at least some effort to return it in one form or another that is useful to the benefactor. Philosophers are in contention as to the dual nature of gratitude, i.e., whether gratitude is primarily a virtue or a duty. Psychologists debate as to whether gratitude is a trait or an attitude. There are also many interrelations between gratitude, duty, justice, and generosity.

Now let us look at the two key players involved in gratitude. The one who gives a gift or does a favor is called the benefactor, and the one who receives it is called the beneficiary. The word benefactor comes from two Latin words *bene* and *facere*, of which the former means "good," and the latter means "to do." So, a benefactor is a person who does something good for the beneficiary. The word "beneficiary" comes from the Latin word *beneficiarius,* which means "one who enjoys a favor." So a beneficiary is somebody who enjoys the kindness or favor.

According to ancient Greek philosophers such as Socrates, Plato, Aristotle, Cicero, and Seneca, gratitude is a virtue, duty, and justice. It is the parent of all virtues as many other virtues sprout from it. A good benefactor is a person who has the best interest of the beneficiary in mind, and the benefactor should not expect anything in return from the beneficiary. The beneficiary should be grateful to the benefactor for the gifts received and should try to make an equal return to the benefactor. According to some of them, gratitude is not required unless the action is supererogatory, i.e., the action is good, but is not morally obligatory. According to Cicero, there is no one in this world who grew up without the kindness of many individuals. He even states that people should be religious and should be grateful to gods for all the goods they have received in this life.

According to St. John Chrysostom, who lived in the fourth century, gratefulness must be shown not in words or tongue, but in deeds and work and in disposition of heart. Gratitude should be shown irrespective of the nature of benefits, i.e., whether the benefit is good or bad, as per the recipient. When parents punish their children, the punishment may be bad according to the judgment of the children, but its goal is the betterment of the children, of which the children may be unaware. A child that appreciates a parent who punishes him is a holy child. He says that a tongue that gives thanks to God in evil circumstances is a holy tongue, and the act is considered equivalent to martyrdom. Therefore, we should thank God not only when life is rosy, but also when it is bleak.

According to St. Ignatius Loyola, ingratitude is the most detestable sin. It is the cause, beginning, and origin of all evils and sins. Acknowledgments of blessings and gifts are received with love and appreciation by the benefactors on earth, and in heaven. Ingratitude is the deadliest sin.

According to St. Thomas Aquinas, gratitude is a special virtue allied with justice. He put down the three rules of gratitude: recognition of the gift, expression of thankfulness, and repayment. Hence, gratitude includes instant acknowledgment of favors received, a thankful disposition of the heart, and an attempt to repay it. A benefactor may not withdraw benefits but may withdraw benefits if the beneficiary is proved ungrateful beyond the benefit of doubt. Since gratitude is a virtue, its opposite, ingratitude, is a vice. Ingratitude, combined with contempt for the duty required by the norms of gratitude, can lead to a mortal sin.

Let us look at some examples. When Alpha gives alms of one dollar to a mendicant in the subway concourse, Alpha is the benefactor, and the mendicant is the beneficiary. Alpha gives the alms expecting nothing in return and he gives it solely with the intention of helping the beneficiary. Here Alpha is an ideal benefactor, and the action is supererogatory as it is something good but not morally required. If Alpha gives the alms *only* to show others that he is a generous person, then the action is not supererogatory as he has a clandestine agenda behind his almsgiving. When receiving alms, the mendicant is supposed to say *thank you* or make a gesture of thankfulness through which he acknowledges the gift. What if he receives alms in his hands, and even without looking at Alpha, turns to another person asking for alms? Then he is ungrateful. Will Alpha give him alms when Alpha sees him a week or month later? If this happens a couple of times, would Alpha ever give him any more alms? This is what St. Thomas meant when he said that when a beneficiary is ungrateful beyond the benefit of doubt, the benefactor will no longer give him anymore gifts.

Look at another example. Bravo had no job and requested Delta to give him a loan of $5,000 without interest to start a business. Delta gave him the loan and Bravo was verbally thankful. The business gradually flourished and Bravo became a millionaire, but Delta lost his job and had difficulty making both ends meet. Bravo repaid Delta the loan which he received from Delta to start the business. Then Bravo cut off all ties with Delta fearing that Delta might ask him for a loan as Delta was not in a good financial situation. Bravo told the world that God blessed him and his business and started to frequent the church to thank God for making him rich. In this case, even though Bravo returned the loan, he was not grateful since he did not demonstrate the right disposition of heart toward the real benefactor and was hypocritical as he assigned his success to God disregarding the manifestation of God in the person of Delta. Here Delta is a benefactor and Bravo is a malevolent and ungrateful beneficiary.

Look at a third example. In a village there was a person named Theta, who lost all his wealth in business. He had a lot of costly silverware and bronzeware at his house. His neighbor, Echo, was a rich person. Whenever Theta needed money to buy food for his children, he would go to Echo and ask for money. Echo knew that Theta could never repay the money. So, whenever Theta asked him for money, Echo would ask for one of the pieces of silverware/bronzeware as collateral. As months passed on, all the costly silverware/bronzeware in Theta's house ended up in Echo's house and they eventually became his property. Was Echo, who helped Theta to buy food for children, a benefactor? Since Echo was acting on his own interest with the covert intention of stealing Theta's silverware/bronzeware for a cheap price, Echo was not a benefactor, but a malefactor.

How about all the favors we receive from God? Do we have to be grateful to God? How do we return God's favor? According to St. Thomas Aquinas, we should acknowledge the gift, have a thankful disposition, and try to repay it. Of course, we can acknowledge the gift by saying a *thank you* from our heart. We can also have a thankful disposition by adoring and praising him for his gift at home or in church. But how do we repay it? God does not need anything. He is fullness in everything. If he needs anything, then he is not God. According to St. Thomas Aquinas, we should repay it through piety, which means that we should return it to his manifestations around us on earth. Therefore, if God has made somebody a rich person, he should show his gratefulness to God not only by going to church every day and by praying with both hands up, but also by sharing that wealth, beginning at home i.e., with parents, children, relatives, the community, the needy in the world, etc.

So, we can show gratitude to God by thanksgiving and sharing with others what he has given us. If only lip service is done, then we are ungrateful, because lip service is easy and we do not help anyone by doing it. When a singer sings and makes people happy, he is sharing his God-given talent with people and is showing his gratitude to God. If he is singing to make reasonable money for his daily living, then also he is using his God-given gift to make his living and repay God by sharing the rest with others. But if he is charging exorbitant amounts per song to become rich, then he is not sharing his God-given ability and is ungrateful to God and is abusing God's gift. If a film actor makes millions of dollars by acting, he may be making people happy, but if he is not sharing his wealth with others and has not been grateful to God for giving him that talent because he does not make a return to God, i.e., his manifestations around him, then he is not only ungrateful, but also malevolent in misusing this gift from God to exploit people. So, we can repay God for the favors he gives us by paying to his needy manifestations (i.e., the poor) right here down on earth.

According to St. Thomas Aquinas, irreligion is a vice stemming from ingratitude to God, who has given us many things out of divine love. According to him, irreligion is denial of the existence of God, refusal to acknowledge the gifts from God, not thanking God for the gifts received, and not trying to repay him through piety. But today's religions are far from the religion of the times of the angelic doctor. That was a time when people worshipped God from the heart, practiced what they prayed, and repaid God or his manifestations (i.e., the poor and the needy), a return for God's gifts. But today, religion has become an easy way to heaven for many. The faithful are given the false assurance that if they pray and support the church financially, they will go to heaven. There is no work or sweating involved in praying. Since many have a lot of time to waste, the praying portion is easy. Supporting the church by giving the weekly collection fulfills the second part of duty to God. But that money is used for maintenance of buildings and the clergy. So, what does God really get and how is he repaid?

According to St. Augustine, the word *religion* comes from the Latin word *religere,* which means "to bind or restrain." Religion is a restraint to bind human souls to God. Consequently, irreligion, for this book, is defined as not believing in the existence of God and not being grateful to God for what he has given us, and not trying to repay God (i.e., his manifestations on earth) according to our capability, irrespective of any affiliation to any of the established religions. It is always good to have membership in, and affiliation with, established religions, so long as they bind souls to God and not to earth.

What about gratefulness to animals? Do we have to be grateful to a dog for giving us company or to a cow for giving us milk? If we do not say *thank you* to dogs or cows, are they going to be upset? As discussed above, gratitude involves rational elements. Animals are not rational beings and they do not have the rationale to understand mental disposition and so gratefulness does not make any sense to a dog or a cow. Moreover, their actions may not be with an intentional disposition to help us. However, we can be thankful to them by taking care of them, by patting them, and by being kind to them. So, we are thankful to the dogs, cows, and other animals, but not grateful to them as they do not have the intention of helping us. But we should always be grateful to God who provided them to us through providence.

What about inanimate entities such as the sun, the earth, rivers, mountains, trees, etc.? They do good things for us. Should we not be grateful? They are inanimate, or without *animus* or mind, and as such they are irrational beings and do not understand mental dispositions. The tree does not give us shade from the sun or produce oxygen for us to breath with any intention of helping us. The mango tree does not produce mangoes with the intention of giving fruits to us. So, gratefulness does not make any sense, yet we can still show our appreciation. Hugging a tree or watering plants show our love for them. But we should be always grateful to God who provided them to us through providence.

According to Maslow's hierarchy of needs, human motivation is guided by a hierarchy of needs. In ascending order, they are the physiological needs, safety and security needs, love and belonging needs, esteem needs, and the need for self-actualization and transcendence. The lower levels must be satisfied before moving to upper levels. According to him, the most basic needs are the physiological needs, i.e., food, shelter, and clothing. But do not overlook or forget some other needs which go before Maslow's hierarchy of needs. First comes our existence itself on earth. Then we need the sun, oxygen, water, and other conditions conducive to survival. Nobody can survive without these. Since existence of the individual itself and the conditions for survival are taken for granted, there is no motivation for humans to be grateful to God, who has provided existence and the necessary conditions for existence. So, we must come out from the mindset of taking things for granted.

Finally, what about gratitude to self? Do we need to be grateful to ourselves? Life is full of twists and turns, so everybody needs to have a guiding principle and a goal outside oneself, and should be striving to achieve that goal or stick to that principle, come what may. Look at history: Socrates was unjustly put to death for alleged corruption of youth; Jesus Christ was unjustly crucified by the displeased Jewish clergy for exposing their hypocrisy; Joan of Arc was unjustly burnt as a heretic; Galileo Galilei died in unjust house arrest for saying that the earth went around the sun; Abraham Lincoln, Mahatma Gandhi, and Martin Luther King were shot dead for standing up for justice. It has been so from time immemorial. They all faced their end courageously because they believed they were doing the right thing.

Even though many of us will not have to undergo such heinous atrocities, we also must face obstacles in life to attain our goals. So, at times it is necessary that we should examine, approve, and reapprove our stand. We should pat ourselves on the back for doing a good job within the limits of the resources given to us by the Almighty. We should be grateful to our inner self for proceeding fearlessly through life even if the whole world is against us, just as Socrates and Jesus Christ did. So, gratitude to oneself and self-approval of our stand are a must for completing our mission too. The failure to be grateful to oneself, from time to time, will end up in irreversible disaster.

In a nutshell, let us conclude that gratitude is a virtue on account of which a person acknowledges the receipt of a useful gift from another, is thankful in heart to the benefactor who gave the gift, and makes some effort to repay it in a form that is useful to the benefactor. The gift should be wanted, accepted, and useful to the beneficiary. Since gratitude is a virtue, its opposite, ingratitude, is a vice. Irreligion is ingratitude to God by avoiding acknowledgment and expression of thankfulness for gifts received from God. Repayment to God is made to his manifestation on earth (i.e., the poor and the needy). Gratitude is closely related to justice. Repayment for gifts received, in a form useful to the benefactor, is a duty, and the omission of such repayment is unjust and is tantamount to dereliction of duty. Gratitude is not owed when the benefactor has clandestine intentions for his generosity. Thankfulness, not gratitude, is owed to animals and inanimate beings as their actions are devoid of intentional mental dispositions. Nothing should be taken for granted, including existence itself and the conditions for our survival. We should also not forget to be grateful to ourselves for doing the best we can with what we have been provided by the Almighty.

Part I

"For you have possessed my temperament.
You have supported me from the womb of my mother.
I will confess to you, for you have been magnified terribly.
Your works are miraculous, as my soul knows exceedingly well.
My bone, which you have made in secret, has not been hidden
from you, and my substance is in accord with the lower parts
of the earth. Your eyes saw my imperfection, and
all this shall be written in your book. Days will be formed,
and no one shall be in them."[1]

1. Ps 138:13–16 (CPDV).

1

Parents: The Ambassadors of God on Earth

How did I wind up on the face of the earth?
Was it mere chance or ruthless destiny?
Or was it the materialization of meticulous planning
and impeccable execution?

I would not have been alive on this beautiful planet:
if my parents did not intend to make me,
if they had used contraceptives to evade me,
if they had not taken care of me in my mother's womb,
if they had not abstained from habits injurious to the unborn,
if they had not realized that I was a gift from God,

Part I

if they had not loved my unseen and unknown face,
if they had aborted me when I was an embryo,
if they had aborted me when I was a fetus,
if they had not taken measures for a safe delivery,
if they had not let the nurse safely usher me into the world,
if they had discarded me to die when I was born,
if they had sold me off when I was born,
if they had turned their backs on me when I was a newborn,
if they had been selfish not to spend their time with me,
if they had been selfish not to spend their wealth on me,
if they had not chosen to sacrifice years of their life for me.

The human baby is the most vulnerable offspring:
A calf can stand, walk, and eat as soon as it is born.
A billy goat can stand and walk as soon as it is born.
Many animal offspring can take care of themselves
with little or no training at all as a newborn,
but not the human baby, which rules the world.
It is incredibly helpless at birth.
It is unbelievably pathetic at birth.
It is unimaginably helpless during the first few years.
It is inconceivably pathetic during the first few years.
Its existence and survival are at the mercy of others.
How easy life would have been for the whole world,
if human babies, as soon as they came out of the womb,
could stand, walk, run, talk, and walk to the
hospital cafeteria to get their first drinks or meals
just as calves, billy goats, and snakelets!

I would not have survived the newborn and toddler ages:
if they had not watched over me day and night,
if they had not watched over me twenty-four-seven,
if they had not watched over me sixty minutes every hour,
if they had not watched over me sixty seconds every minute,
if they had not watched every movement of mine,
if they had turned their back on me even for a minute,

as I lay in the crib like a helpless, inanimate toy,
or while exploring the world by crawling and toddling,
putting into my mouth everything I could lay my hands on.

They fed and nourished me as needed:
They fed me using feeding bottles.
They then taught me how to feed myself from bottles.
They fed me using their fingers.
They then taught me to feed myself with my own hands.
They fed me using spoons.
They then taught me how to feed myself with spoons.
They then taught me how to eat with spoon and fork.
They then taught me how to eat with spoon, fork, and knife.
They transitioned my food from liquid to pureed.
They transitioned my food from pureed to chunk.
They transitioned my food from chunk to table food.
They transitioned my food from their choice to my choice.

They were with me like my midday shadow:
They watched over me when I tried to hold my head up.
They watched over me when I rocked side to side.
They watched over me when I rolled over, belly to back.
They watched over me when I rolled over, back to belly.
They watched over me when I first sat up.
They watched over me when I started to crawl.
They watched over me when I tried to sit up.
They watched over me when I tried to stand up.
They watched over me when I began to stand alone.
They watched over me when I tried my first steps.
They watched over me when I walked, holding furniture.
They watched over me when I staggered and fell.
They watched me over when I started to run around.
They carried me in their arms and hips.
They carried me on their shoulders and head.

They rocked me to sleep with lullabies.
They watched me through baby monitors while asleep.

Part I

They were right in front of me whenever I woke up,
as if they were the sentries of my regal sleep.
They were at arm's length from me, in my infancy.
They kept an eye on me in my childhood.
They were watching me in my adolescence.
They taught me to tell the truth always.
They brought me up in their religion.
They taught me how to be a good citizen.
They did not let me grow up on the streets.
They did not throw me into an orphanage.
They gave me food when I was hungry.
They provided me shelter, which I always needed.
They bought me clothes that they could afford.
They took me to doctors when I was sick.

They sent me to school so I could learn.
They did not spare the rod and spoil me.
They armored me with education and perseverance,
and not with guns or knives or arrogance.
They sheathed me with patience and endurance,
and not with impatience and intolerance.
They educated me to make me self-sufficient.
They made the scaffold for my independence.
They made the scaffold for my self-sufficiency.
They protected me from all kinds of dangers,
even at the risk of their own lives.
They took care of me as the apple of their eyes.
They molded me from nothingness.
When they were convinced that I could sail myself
in the rough and tempestuous world outside,
they let their reins go and launched me off,
yet they kept an eye on me through their binoculars
to make sure I was safe from pirates.

Gratitude is the mother of virtues.
If there is no mother, there are no children.

Ingratitude is a vice, as gratitude is a virtue.
Ingratitude toward God or man in any form is a vice.
Ingratitude toward God is called irreligion.
Ingratitude entails dereliction of duty.
Ingratitude entails unpaid debt.
Ingratitude entails covert injustice.
Ingratitude entails obliquity.
Ingratitude entails narcissism,
which eventually hurls one into dire desolation.
Let me not be ungrateful!

What can I return to my parents
for giving me this wonderful life
and for doing their best to make me my best?
What can I return to you, my Lord and my God,
for giving me this wonderful life through my parents?

Turn away your eyes from my sins:
of breaking your first and third commandments
by not acknowledging your gift of parents,
and of breaking your fourth commandment
by not acknowledging what my parents have done for me,
and by disobedience and by not returning
the debt to them through filial piety.

Grant me the grace to see you in them
and to accept their will as that of yours.
Grant me the grace not to turn my back on them
when they revert to their second infancy.
Grant me the grace to comprehend
the depth of their love that revolved around me.
Grant me the grace to see your face
in the face of admonishing parents and clerics.
Grant me the grace to hear you
through the voices of advising parents and teachers.
Grant me the grace to understand their self-immolation

of sacrificing two to three decades of their life for me.
Grant me the will and strength to take care of them
just as they took care of me in my infancy,
as care is needed at both ends of life
and thus, I may show them my gratitude
for giving me a chance to have this beautiful life.

Grant me the grace to understand that being born
was neither my choice, nor my merit, but their gift to me.
Grant me the grace to understand that being born and
brought up was neither my entitlement nor my prerogative.
Grant me the grace to play the parent role
in my own life down on earth.
Grant me the good will to give an unborn child
a chance to be born into this world.
Grant me the courage to sacrifice part of my life to give
another a chance on this wonderful and beautiful land.
Grant me the grace to work hard to rear my children
and not make them grow up on the streets.
Grant me the grace to overcome selfishness
barring me from making and rearing children for God.
Grant me the grace to be a procreator
and not a disowner or destroyer of life.
Grant me the grace to follow my parents' guidance
rather than that of hedonistic friends
which is tantamount to the blind following the blind.
Grant me the grace to seek and do your will
by seeking and doing the will of my parents,
as they are your ambassadors on earth,
your celestial diplomats to my mundane life.

What thanks can I offer you, my Lord and my God,
for your wonderful gift of parents
as a boon out of your love and mercy?
I will laud your name, my Lord and my God,
I will chant and applaud your name forever!

2

The Traditional Family: The Heaven on Earth

Family is the first society on earth:
It is the basic unit of all larger societies.

Part I

It is the cornerstone of any community.
It is the cornerstone of any county.
It is the cornerstone of any state.
It is the cornerstone of any country.
It is the cornerstone of the world.
It is where the first shelter is provided.
It is the first line of defense for its members.
It is a country in miniscule form, with all portfolios,
including budget, defense, judiciary, and administration.
It is where procreation is carried out.
It is where children are nurtured.
It is where children are oriented.
It is where right and wrong are taught.
It is where the foundation for character is laid.
It is where conduct is formed.
It is where future citizens are molded.
It is where trust is infused and maintained.
It is the school of schools.

It is a unique place in the world:
where heaven and earth meet,
where there are no secrets,
where all services are free of charge,
where members care for one another,
where intimacy, love, and trust are fostered,
where compensatory services are not expected,
where welfare of others stands first in the line,
and welfare of self has the last place in line,
where there are no individual bank accounts,
where loans are given without any collateral,
where loans need not be repaid,
where everyone has the same menu,
where the pain of one pains others,
where happiness of one makes others happy,
where the fall of one is fall of all,
where the rise of one is the rise of all,

where sacrifice is the sword,
where patience is the armor,
where the loser is the real winner,
where the winner is the real loser,
where selfishness has no place,
where ego has no place,
where might is not right,
where narcissism has no place,
where delinquency has no place,
where needs prevail over wants,
where caring and sharing clasp hands,
where *my* is not found in the dictionary,
where *your* is not found in the dictionary,
where *my* and *your* are replaced by *our*,
where the parents are the paragon of sacrifice,
and children are the paragon of trust.
Societies with such families are founded on rock.

The place where family resides is called home:
It is the cradle of character formation.
It is the cradle of enculturation and orientation.
It is the school of schools, where the twig is bent,
deciding how the human tree should grow.
It is the marshalling area before going to the
outside world of the minefield of treacheries.
It is where one can lay one's head down
and sleep all night without the fear of the enemy.
It is where one can rest without fearing ambushes.
It is where one can find oneself most comfortable.
It is where one can find serenity and peace,
even amidst adversity and impoverishment.
It is the only place where we need no sentries.
It is the only place where everything is unlocked.
It is the only place where everything is free.
It is the only place without rent and utility bills.
It is the only place we trust that we are covered.

There is no place like home in the vast universe,
and that is why it is called home.
It is where one feels safe and comfortable,
a place where one's heart is.

Should I not thank my beautiful home,
where all my reminiscences sleep in beauty,
where I wish I were reborn and could repeat myself?
Let me thank all who were in that little home,
who were the matter and form of my home,
which made me who I am and what I am.

Bricks, stones, and mortar do not make a home.
Columns, beams, and welds do not make a home.
Rafters, struts, and kingposts do not make a home.
Roof shingles and vinyl sidings do not make a home.
Porches, decks, and rooms do not make a home.
All the above make what is called a house.
A house where the traditional family lives is a home.
That home is made of love and sacrifice.
It is made of understanding and forgiveness.
It is made of intimacy and trust.
It is made of gratitude and persistence.
It is made of austere souls of love
who are the gifts of God from above.

Gratitude is the mother of virtues.
If there is no mother, there are no children.
Ingratitude is a vice, as gratitude is a virtue.
Ingratitude toward God or man in any form is a vice.
Ingratitude toward God is called irreligion.
Ingratitude entails dereliction of duty.
Ingratitude entails unpaid debt.
Ingratitude entails covert injustice.
Ingratitude entails obliquity.
Ingratitude entails narcissism,

which eventually hurls one into dire desolation.
Let me not be ungrateful!

What can I return to those who made my house a home?
What can I return to you, my Lord and my God,
for giving me a beautiful house with angelic souls
who did their best to make my house a home for me?

Turn away your eyes from my sins against
the immaculate society on earth, i.e., home,
by breaking thy commandments,
such as the first and the third by not acknowledging
your wonderful gift of home which
you freely gave me out of divine love and charity,
the fourth by hindering procreation
and by not respecting parents and overlooking
the education of children, and by not providing
support for parents in their old age,
the fifth by abortion, infanticide, and euthanasia,
the sixth by sins against chastity such as free union,
separation, divorce, infidelity, and same-sex marriages,
and the seventh by switching affection due to humans
to pets by forming new families comprised of
one human being and one or more pets.
Grant me the grace to see Your face
on the faces of others in my home.
Grant me the grace to stay away from all evil forces
which put asunder the unity of home,
such as abortion, infanticide, free union,
abandonment, cohabitation, separation, divorce,
same-sex marriage, and individualism.
Grant me the grace not to have separate bank accounts
for the spouses, which is a sign of distrust.
Grant me the grace not to get rent and share of utility
from my kids staying home after the age of eighteen
which is a sign of selfishness and lack of true love.

Part I

Grant me the grace not to kick children out of home
when they finish their high school as if
they completed PhDs and are self-sufficient.
Grant me the grace to discern that if I love myself
more than my children and spouse
then the family will disintegrate into pieces.
Grant me the grace to spend all my savings
to help my children settle down in life
rather than to hold on to it to my grave.

Grant me the grace not to be a parasite,
living on parents after I pass my mid-twenties.
Grant me the grace not to vie for my parents' estates,
as these are not the product of my toil.
Grant me the grace not to sit down and calculate
my gains or losses in the parent-child transaction,
as no return is enough to equal the gift of life.
Grant me the grace not to redefine family
as consisting of only self, spouse, and children
kicking out everyone else, such as parents and
grandparents, as they are potential liabilities.
Grant me the grace to understand that
charity begins at home and that the
charity that does not begin at home is vanity.
Grant me the grace to help my parents to buy Albuterol
before I donate to orphanages and churches.
Grant me the grace not to discard parents as lemon rinds
after all the juice has been squeezed out of them.
Grant me the grace not to redefine family
with evil social sins of free union, cohabitation, and the like,
which are the signs of hedonism and selfishness
and are tantamount to trying out ready-made dresses
in department stores to see whether they fit me well,
or wearing them for a while and returning them
for another one, saying that they do not fit me well.

What thanks can I offer you, my Lord and my God,
for your wonderful gift of home
as a boon out of your love and mercy!
I will laud your name, my Lord and my God,
I will chant and applaud your name forever.

3

Born Healthy: The Greatest Boon

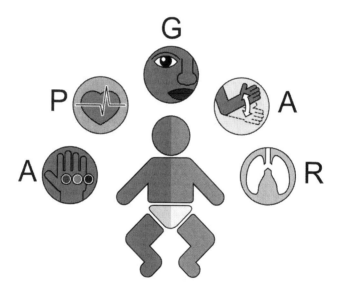

If I were born healthy, it was not my choice.
If I were born healthy, it was not due to my merit.
So why am I indifferent when I am born healthy?
How could I take it for granted
that I should be born healthy?

What if I were born with Down syndrome?
Then I would have physical disabilities,
mental retardation, and developmental problems,
and I would be like a nine-year-old,
needing care all my life
as the genetic disorder has no known cure.

What if I were born with spina bifida?
Then I might be held captive to paralysis.
I could have movement challenges,
and problems with seeing and learning,
and bowl and bladder issues all my life
as there is no cure for this genetic deformity.

What if I were born with autism?
As the word itself indicates,
I would withdraw to myself,
interested only in repetitive behaviors,
disregard the world around me,
ostracize myself from society,
impede my education and development
and I would not be able to lead a normal life.

What if I were born with cerebral palsy?
Then I would have floppy or rigid limbs,
and I would not be able to move as I want,
due to involuntary motions and reflexes,
and I would have problems balancing myself,
leaving me unable to take care of myself.

What if I were born with cystic fibrosis?
Then I would be inundated with lung infections,
and would not be able breath normally,
leaving me with a shorter span of life.

What if I were born with hydrocephalus?
Then I would be physically and mentally inept.
Neither would I be able to balance myself,
nor would I be able to learn as others do,
rendering me unable to take care of myself.

What if I were born with club foot?
Then I would have to walk on one side of my foot
all the days of my life wherever I go.

What if I were born with Amyotrophic Lateral Sclerosis?
Then I would have weakness of muscles,
and I would not be able to do many jobs,
and I would not be cured of it all my life,
making me a burden for the world around me.

What if I were born blind?
Then light and darkness would be the same for me.
I could neither enjoy my life as I do now,
nor could I survive without the mercy of others.

What if I were born deaf and mute?
Then I would be ostracized in this world,
with no easy way to learn or communicate.

If I were born with physical disabilities,
it was neither my choice nor my demerit.
If I were born with mental abnormalities,
it was neither my choice nor my demerit.

Gratitude is the mother of virtues.
If there is no mother, there are no children.
Ingratitude is a vice, as gratitude is a virtue.
Ingratitude toward God or man in any form is a vice.
Ingratitude toward God is called irreligion.
Ingratitude entails dereliction of duty.

Ingratitude entails unpaid debt.
Ingratitude entails covert injustice.
Ingratitude entails obliquity.
Ingratitude entails narcissism,
which eventually hurls one into dire desolation.
Let me not be ungrateful!

What can I return to my parents, my Lord and my God,
for doing their part to make me a healthy newborn?
What can I return to you, my Lord and my God,
for creating me without any congenital deformity?

Turn away your eyes from my sins:
of breaking your first and third commandments
by my ingratitude of not acknowledging
the blessings you showered on me when I was born
which you freely gave me out of divine charity.

Grant me the grace not to take it for granted
that I was born without down syndrome.
Grant me the grace to thank you for your bounty
when I see somebody with autism.
Grant me the grace not to take it for granted
that I was born without cerebral palsy.
Grant me the grace to thank you for your bounty
when I see somebody with cystic fibrosis.
Grant me the grace not to take it for granted
that I was born without hydrocephalus.
Grant me the grace to thank you for your bounty
that I was born without club foot.
Grant me the grace to see how good you were to me
when I see somebody with congenital deformity.

Grant me the grace not to take it for granted
that I was born as a normal child.
Grant me the grace to comprehend that

my parents adopted healthy lifestyles
that were conducive to me while I was in the womb.
Grant me the grace to be grateful to my parents
who went through a different type of nine-month Lent
to do their part to make me a healthy newborn.
Grant me the grace to understand that
being born with sound body and mind
was not an entitlement or privilege,
but it was a gracious boon from earth and heaven.

If I were born with congenital deformities
of physical or mental illness,
then I would be the special one of God.
He has deputed me with a special role
upon this terrestrial sphere.
In his infinite knowledge and wisdom,
with his infinite justice and love,
he loved and trusted me more than anyone else
with this herculean job
to make the world understand the value of the gifts
he has showered freely on all of them.
He has wonderfully knit me in my mother's womb
to carry out his special plan for me on earth.
I am glad that he trusted me with such a great task,
and I will execute it to the best of my ability
so that I do not fall short of his expectations of me.

What thanks can I offer you, my Lord and my God,
for creating me the way that I am
as a boon out of your love and mercy?
I will laud your name, my Lord and my God,
I will chant and applaud your name forever.

4

Time: The Nonexistent Existent

Is time real or unreal, or is it imaginary?
Is it linear or cyclical, or physical or mental?
Does it flow from past to present to future,
or does it flow from future to present to past?
Is it a distention of the human mind?
Is it the fourth dimension of the universe?
Some say we can travel back and forth in time,
if the universe were ten-dimensional as some think.

Did God create time at the time of creation,
or was it there from time immemorial?
The past is past and is there no more.

Part I

The future is not guaranteed to come at all.
The present is evanescent.
All that is there is the fleeting, fleeting *now,*
which is gone before it is thought and said,
and it comes from nothingness
and vanishes into nothingness.

Time, the unseen, intangible phenomenon
we measure in seconds, minutes, hours, days,
weeks, months, years, and so on.
We are born in time and we die in time.
The average span of life is three score and ten.
Have we ever thought about the One
who gives us time or takes it away from us,
the one who decides the span of our time on earth?
Did we buy our time here or did someone
give us as a boon to let us have it free?
Neither did we buy it, nor can we sell it.
It is given to us as an unpredictable, contingent gift.

We have no control over time and our life span.
Some die in the womb of their mother.
Some die as they are born into the world.
Some die as infants and some as toddlers.
Some die as children and some as teenagers.
Some die in adolescence and in early adulthood.
Some die in adulthood in the prime of life.
Some die when they are the youngest old.
Some die when they are middle old.
Some die when they are the oldest old.
And some die after hitting a century.

How blessed am I when I am reading this?
I am enjoying the life given to me as a boon.
I am enjoying the years I did not buy.
I am enjoying the months I did not buy.

I am enjoying the day I did not buy.
I am enjoying the hour I did not buy.
I am enjoying the minute I did not buy.
I am enjoying the second I did not buy.
I am enjoying the fleeting *now*s,
which are as unpredictable as the drops of water
that trickle down from the icicles on a tree branch,
which may or may not trickle down,
which may or may not reach the ground.

People spend millions and millions of dollars
to buy one more day of life to live.
They stake everything they have at hand
to live a day more or even an hour more.
Even those saintly people who know well
that when they die, they will go to heaven,
do never wish to die and go sooner to heaven,
because life here is more precious than in heaven.
This shows that time is such a precious thing,
that even all the wealth of the whole universe
cannot buy one nanosecond of this precious gem.

Life is measured in years and years in months,
and months in weeks and weeks in days,
and days in hours and hours in minutes,
and minutes in seconds and the seconds
are made of the fleeting, unpredictable *now*s.

To make the long story short, life is made of time,
and so, time is life and life is time.
Wasting my time is killing my time,
and killing my time is killing my life,
and killing my life is called suicide,
which is against the fifth commandment.

Part I

Yet, do I live as if the days of my life are eternal,
not thinking about the preciousness of time,
and waste this precious time lying down idly all day long,
or watching entertainments day in and day out,
or wasting time at my work by cutting corners on jobs,
thus, stealing time from my employer's pocket,
or wasting time at school daydreaming in class,
thus, stealing time of my parents who worked long hours
to make money to send me to school,
and stealing it from teachers who spent their time
preparing for teaching me at school?
These are all breaches of the seventh commandment.

Time is a coin that is given to me to prove myself.
Whatever time I have been given by God,
I must give return for each and every second
that has been given to me without any excuse.
I am the steward of time given to me by God,
and wasting it is an incorrigible breach
of the fifth and the seventh commandments.

So, should I not think a million times
"How am I spending my time?"
just as I think "How shall I spend my money
so that I do not stake it or waste it
from day to day so that I don't run out of it?"

Gratitude is the mother of virtues.
If there is no mother, there are no children.
Ingratitude is a vice, as gratitude is a virtue.
Ingratitude toward God or man in any form is a vice.
Ingratitude toward God is called irreligion.
Ingratitude entails dereliction of duty.
Ingratitude entails unpaid debt.
Ingratitude entails covert injustice.
Ingratitude entails obliquity.

Ingratitude entails narcissism,
which eventually hurls one into dire desolation.
Let me not be ungrateful!

What can I return to my parents, my Lord and my God,
for giving me a chance to initiate my time?
What can I return to you, my Lord and my God,
for giving me so many years of life?

Turn away your eyes from my sins:
of breaking your first commandment through sloth,
of breaking your first and third commandments
by my ingratitude of not acknowledging
what you gave me freely out of divine charity,
of breaking the fifth commandment by killing time,
and of breaking the seventh by stealing time.

Grant me the grace to thank God before I go to sleep
for giving me one more night to sleep in peace.
Grant me the grace to thank God when I wake at dawn
for giving me one more precious day to live, a day
that cannot be bought with all the wealth of the world.
Grant me the grace to thank God when I blow out the candles
on my birthdays for keeping me safe in the bygone year.
Grant me the grace to thank God when I blow out the candles
on my birthdays for giving me more time to live.
Grant me the grace to invoke his blessings for days to come
when I blow out my birthday candles.

Grant me the grace not to squander time.
Grant me the grace to not let time be
like pearls thrown before pigs.
Grant me the grace not to commit the capital sin of sloth
by wasting the precious time you give me.
Grant me the grace not to waste my time
by watching sports from morn to night

or by watching movies from night to morn.
Grant me the grace not to waste my time
by sitting idle on my porch, watching passersby.
Grant me the grace not to waste my time
by building castles in the air rather than working.
Grant me the grace not to steal anyone's time,
whether it is at work or at school or somewhere else.
Grant me the grace to think that
every day is a free boon from You.
Grant me the grace to understand that
it is a precious gift from God.
Grant me the grace to perceive that
God has given it to me out of love.
Grant me the grace to realize that
many yearned for it, but did not get it.

Grant me the grace not to take the next year for granted.
Grant me the grace not to take the next month for granted.
Grant me the grace not to take the next week for granted.
Grant me the grace not to take tomorrow for granted.
Grant me the grace not to take the next hour for granted.
Grant me the grace not to take the next minute for granted.
Grant me the grace not to postpone anything for tomorrow,
if I can find a minute or two to do it today,
not because procrastination is an evil to success,
but because it lets the capital sin of sloth creep into me.
Give me the grace to do *now* everything that I would do
if I knew I am going to die in an hour or a day,
for I do not know the hour or the day the Lord comes,
just as the goat that is being taken into a butcher shop
knows not the hour the axe is going to fall on its neck.

Grant me the grace not to build a bungalow
for this evanescent life, which needs only a tent.
Grant me the grace not to hoard for years to come
when even the next second is not assured.

Grant me the grace to live with the thought that the
unwelcome guest of death may beckon me at any time.
Grant me the grace to be grateful to the Almighty,
who grants me time, second by second,
so that he does not stop giving that to me
because of my sheer ungratefulness.

What thanks can I offer you, my Lord and my God,
for giving me so many precious years of life
as a boon out of your love and mercy?
I will laud your name, my Lord and my God,
I will chant and applaud your name forever.

5

The Eyes: The Most Delightful Sense

The human eye, the most complex part
of the human body, second only to the brain,
with its multiple layers, and interconnections,
with millions of working parts,
with an iris that is unique for each human being,
is the masterpiece of an infinite intelligence.

Its diameter is less than an inch, but

its accomplishments are beyond the wildest imaginations.
The whole visible universe of unimaginable size
can be squeezed inside this one-inch ball,
which is like squeezing the whole earth
inside a tiny mustard seed.
Its design is the work of infinite intelligence.

It can see the horizon at three miles on level ground.
It can see a candle flickering two miles away.
It can see mountains one hundred miles away.
It can see six thousand stars in a clear sky.
The naked eye can see many galaxies
which are quintillions of miles away.
It can distinguish ten million different colors.
It brings us eighty percent of all information taken in.

Think about being born and living without eyes:
We would not be able to learn anything by reading.
We would not be able to see the sun or the moon or the sky.
We would not be able to enjoy the sunrise or the sunset.
We would not be able to enjoy the beauty of moonlit nature.
We would not be able to enjoy the starry sky at night.
We would not be able to see the beauty of the twinkling stars.
We would not be able to gaze into the cerulean sky.
We would not be able to see the beauty of mountain ranges.
We would not be able to see the beauty of lush, verdant valleys.
We would not be able to see the hills or dales or ridges.
We would not be able to see the hummocks or hillocks anymore.
We would not be able to see rainbows.
We would not be able to see the sunset or the sunrise.
We would not be able to see the beautiful scenery of nature.

We would not be able to see the different colors of flowers.
We would not be able to see different types of trees or bushes.
We would not be able to see different colors of autumn leaves.
We would not be able to see the lightning or the rain.

We would not be able to see the hail or the snow.
We would not be able to see the food or drink we ingest.
We would not be able to see planes or cars or bicycles.
We would not be able to watch movies or games.
We would not be able to see dogs, cats, cows, or hens.
We would not be able to see what our house looks like.
We would not be able to see our beloved parents and siblings.

Everything would be pitch dark around us.
We would not be able to see the road ahead of us.
We would not be able to see the wall in front of us.
We would not be able to see a gorge waiting ahead for us.

As we would be blind to the future ahead of us,
those who are born and live blind
are blind to the world around them.
It is an unknown and unseen world for them
just as the future is unknown to us.

Am I not blessed that I am born with two good eyes?
Did I purchase my vision from someone?
I know that I did not,
rather, I was born with two good eyes.

Should I not be thankful to someone for these
priceless eyes which were given to me free?
When I see with my eyes, do I thank God
for giving me such wonderful eyes?

Gratitude is the mother of virtues.
If there is no mother, there are no children.
Ingratitude is a vice, as gratitude is a virtue.
Ingratitude toward God or man in any form is a vice.
Ingratitude toward God is called irreligion.
Ingratitude entails dereliction of duty.
Ingratitude entails unpaid debt.

The Eyes: The Most Delightful Sense

Ingratitude entails covert injustice.
Ingratitude entails obliquity.
Ingratitude entails narcissism,
which eventually hurls one into dire desolation.
Let me not be ungrateful!

What can I return to you, my Lord and my God,
for giving me the most delightful sense of sight through my eyes,
which you have designed with such sophistication
that the whole universe can be seen in them?

Turn away your eyes from my ocular sins
of initiating breeches of thy commandments:
such as the first and third by not acknowledging
the eyes you freely gave me out of divine charity,
the second by false oaths and perjury,
the fourth by closing my eyes on parents and family
when I do not need their help anymore,
the fifth by scandal and intemperance,
the sixth through the lust of eyes,
the seventh by not seeing thee in the poor,
the eighth by false witnessing and perjury,
the ninth by the lust of the eyes and voyeurism,
and the tenth by envy and coveting the things of others.

Grant me the grace to thank God for my priceless eyes:
when I read books,
when I enjoy movies and entertainment,
when I see my loved ones,
when I see the beauty of nature,
when I make my daily living,
when I see a blind person,
when I see a person walking with a white cane.

Grant me the grace to appreciate beauty,
but not to be vanquished by it.

Grant me the grace to dream on the beauty of angels
when I see beautiful lasses and handsome lads.
Grant me the grace always to keep in mind
that beauty is skin-deep and not a substantial attribute.
Grant me the grace not to fall into the capital sins
of the lust of the eyes and of greed.
Grant me the grace not to be a scandal to others
in churches, shopping malls, and public places,
by presenting myself half-clothed.

Grant me the grace not to fall into the capital sins
of covetousness and envy, which enter through my eyes.
Grant me the grace not to put blame on you, Lord,
for not creating me with eyes in the back of my head, too.
Grant me the grace not to bear false witness
by telling what I did not see.
Grant me the grace not to bear false witness
by not telling what I saw.
Grant me the grace to tell the truth
that has entered through my eyes.
Grant me the grace to open my eyes
to see the poor and needy around me.
Grant me the grace to open my eyes
to see you in the needy around me.
Grant me the grace to enjoy another's rise
and not to rejoice at another's fall.
Grant me the grace not to be greedy,
but to be content with what I have.
Grant me the grace to acknowledge that
my eyes are a free boon from God.
Grant me the grace to acknowledge that
God has given it to me out of love.
Grant me the grace to acknowledge that
many yearned for it, but did not get it.
Grant me the grace to acknowledge that
I should not take my vision for granted.

The Eyes: The Most Delightful Sense

What thanks can I offer you, my Lord and my God,
for giving me priceless, precious eyes
as a boon out of your love and mercy?
I will laud your name, my Lord and my God,
I will chant and applaud your name forever.

6

Speech and Hearing: The Bridge to People

The faculties of speech and hearing are a bridge
that connects human beings.
Without speech and hearing,
we are like islands in an archipelago,
with no connection or communication.

Imagine a life without the sense of hearing:
We would not be able to attend to a phone call.

Speech and Hearing: The Bridge to People

We would not be able to learn anything from our parents.
We would not be able to learn anything from our teachers.
We would not be able to learn anything from our clergy.
We would not be able to hear our siblings or friends.
We would not be able to hear the alarm in the morning.
We would not be able to hear the church bells ringing .
We would not be able to communicate with physicians.
We would not be able to sleep hearing lullabies.
We would not be able to listen to nostalgic songs anymore.
We would not be able to listen to concerts anymore.
We would not be able to enjoy movies anymore.
We would not be able to enjoy songs and the sounds of birds.
We would not be able to enjoy the burbling of streams.
We would not be able to enjoy the roaring of beach waves.

Hearing saves our lives many a time.
Our lives would have been much shorter
if we did not have ears to hear:
The trumpeting of elephants warns us to be cautious.
The bellowing of alligators warns us to be cautious.
The roaring of tigers warns us to be cautious.
The barking of dogs warns us to be cautious.
The buzzing of hornets tells us to watch out.
The hissing of snakes warns us of danger.
The sound of lighting tells us to take cover.
The sound of a gun warns us of danger.
The sound of footsteps warns of an approaching person.
The sound of a collision warns us of accidents.
The beeping sound of a horn tells us to be alert.
The civil sirens tell us of impending danger.

If we are mute, we cannot talk to anyone:
We cannot talk to parents or siblings.
We cannot talk to teachers or doctors.
We cannot talk to peers or friends.
We cannot make a phone call.

We cannot sing or hum a song.
We cannot have any communication
with the outside world and that cuts us off
from a normal social life.

Gratitude is the mother of virtues.
If there is no mother, there are no children.
Ingratitude is a vice, as gratitude is a virtue.
Ingratitude toward God or man in any form is a vice.
Ingratitude toward God is called irreligion.
Ingratitude entails dereliction of duty.
Ingratitude entails unpaid debt.
Ingratitude entails covert injustice.
Ingratitude entails obliquity.
Ingratitude entails narcissism,
which eventually hurls one into dire desolation.
Let me not be ungrateful!

What can I return to You, my Lord and my God,
for giving me the abilities of speech and hearing,
which you have designed ingeniously
to help me to traverse this rough terrain of life?

Turn away your eyes from my sins of initiating
breeches of thy commandments with my tongue and ears:
such as the first by ingratitude, divination, or heresy,
the second by blasphemy, or perjury, or
by adopting pseudo names to hide Christian identity,
the third by ingratitude to God by not thanking him
for the gifts of speech and hearing,
the fourth by not listening to parents, elders, and clergy,
the fifth by verbal violence, altercations, threats,
and supporting pro-choice movements,
the sixth by seducing and being seduced,
the seventh by eavesdropping and breaking promises,
the eighth by bearing false witness,

or engaging in perjury, judgment, slander, and boasting,
the ninth by having an unchaste tongue,
and the tenth by initiating theft and fraud.

Grant me the grace not to use my tongue
to pray as a goods train without internal disposition.
Grant me the grace not to use my tongue
for divination, heresy, or blasphemy.
Grant me the grace not to use my tongue
for perjury, slander, or lying.
Grant me the grace not to turn a deaf ear
to parents, elders, teachers, and clergy.
Grant me the grace not to hurt the feelings
of others with words that cannot be retracted.
Grant me the grace to think thrice before I speak
as words are like bullets from a pistol.
Grant me the grace to discern that the tongue
can turn heaven into hell and vice versa.
Grant me the grace to understand that the tongue
is the root cause of all evils in the world.
Grant me the grace to meditate on the fact that
the wounds made by the tongue fester like a sore
to such an extent that the old saying
time heals all wounds does not hold water
as they may sometimes follow one even to the grave.

Grant me the grace not to kill justice in courts of law
by asking and demanding a witness to say only *yes* or *no*
where neither *yes* nor *no* is the truth,
thus barring the sworn witness from telling the truth
and making the sworn witness commit forced perjury
and cutting the throat of justice itself right at the court.
Grant me the grace to acknowledge that
my speech is a free boon from above.
Grant me the grace to acknowledge that
speech and hearing are a precious gift from God.

Part I

Grant me the grace not to hurt with my tongue
the Lord who gave me the faculty of speech.
Grant me the grace not to take these faculties for granted.

What thanks can I offer you, my Lord and my God,
for giving me the faculties of speech and hearing
as a boon out of your love and mercy?
I will laud your name, my Lord and my God,
I will chant and applaud your name forever.

7

Taste: The Most Enjoyed Sense

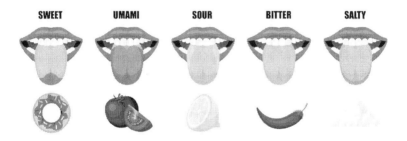

| SWEET | UMAMI | SOUR | BITTER | SALTY |

Taste is a great gift which lures and entices us
to eat and drink to maintain our bodily systems.
There are thousands of taste buds on the tongue
and many combinations of tastes.

How boring and tedious would eating be:
if mangoes and apples were tasteless like water
if cherries and oranges were tasteless like water
if grapes and avocados were tasteless like water
if figs and dates were tasteless like water
if blueberries and grapes were tasteless like water
if jackfruits and pineapples were tasteless like water
if asparagus and beans were tasteless like water
if onion and pepper were tasteless like water

Part I

if tomato and potato were tasteless like water
if yam and lettuce were tasteless like water
if fish and pork were tasteless like water
if pizza and hamburgers were tasteless like water
if crab and sushi were tasteless like water
if tandoori chicken and steak were tasteless like water
if fish korma and beef curry were tasteless like water
if Continental, European, Mexican, Indian, and Italian
cuisines all tasted the same as tasteless water?

How boring would be drinking:
if Coca-Cola and Pepsi were savorless
if Tropicana and Fanta were savorless
if Gatorade and Sprite were savorless
if Nescafe and Folgers were savorless
if cappuccinos and lattes were savorless
if whisky and rum were savorless
if gin and vodka were savorless
if martini and champagne were savorless
if Long Island iced teas and brandy were savorless
if red wine and white wine were savorless?

There was a resident in a nursing home
who was in bed after an abdominal surgery.
He had a postsurgical feeding tube
and when he was told that the feeding tube
must be there for the rest of his life,
he told the doctor to take it away
and refused all types of parenteral nutrition.
He would rather die than live without eating,
for that was the only thing he enjoyed in life.
We already know that some eat to live
and there are some who live to eat.

Should I not appreciate the sense of taste
so ingeniously designed into my making

so that it makes life enjoyable on earth?
The taste buds make eating pleasurable.
It is an indispensable simple pleasure
that every human on earth enjoys,
for there lives no human being
who does not enjoy a luscious meal,
be they a beggar or a king.

Gratitude is the mother of virtues.
If there is no mother, there are no children.
Ingratitude is a vice, as gratitude is a virtue.
Ingratitude toward God or man in any form is a vice.
Ingratitude toward God is called irreligion.
Ingratitude entails dereliction of duty.
Ingratitude entails unpaid debt.
Ingratitude entails covert injustice.
Ingratitude entails obliquity.
Ingratitude entails narcissism,
which eventually hurls one into dire desolation.
Let me not be ungrateful!

What can I return to you, my Lord and my God,
for giving me the much-needed sense of taste,
so ingeniously designed to entice me to eat and drink
to enable me to stay alive in this beautiful world?

Turn away your eyes from my sins
of breaking thy commandments:
such as the first and the third by not acknowledging
the wonderful gift of taste which
you freely gave me out of divine charity,
the fifth by intemperate use of
food, drugs, alcohol, and medicines,
which is detrimental to life,
and the seventh by wasting food,
by making more than is needed.

Part I

Grant me the grace to thank you for the food
on the table before every meal I take.
Grant me the grace to thank you for the food
after every meal I take.
Grant me the grace to thank all who worked
behind the curtain to bring food to my table
from farmers to truck drivers, to the cook and servers.
Grant me the grace to keep in mind that
hundreds of hands worked behind the food I eat.
Grant me the grace not to waste any food
as the food I waste may be tasty to the hungry.

Grant me the grace not to fall into
the capital sin of gluttony by eating
luxurious, exotic, and costly food.
Grant me the grace not to be a glutton,
by eating more than is needed.
Grant me the grace not to be a glutton,
by eating with haste and greed.
Grant me the grace not to be a glutton,
by eating out of time just for fun.
Grant me the grace not to be a glutton,
by eating just to satisfy my appetite.
Grant me the grace not to be a glutton
by eating elaborately prepared food.
Grant me the grace not to be a glutton,
by eating just for sensual gratification
and to appease the vile sense of taste.

Grant me the grace to be happy with the taste
of the food I eat, without complaining.
Grant me the grace not to be like a five-year-old,
pushing away plates that are not pleasurable.
Grant me the grace not to be a wastrel,
spending one hundred dollars for a meal
when I can do it for twenty dollars.

Taste: The Most Enjoyed Sense

Grant me the grace to share my food
with those who are starving.

What thanks can I offer you, my Lord and my God,
for giving me the wonderful gift of taste
as a boon out of your love and mercy?
I will laud your name, my Lord and my God,
I will chant and applaud your name forever.

8

The Sense of Smell: The Chimney of Relations

Smell is a life-saving sense.
It is vital for human survival.
It helps us to know the presence of hazards.
It saves us from impending dangers.
It helps us in many ways in our daily life.

The smell of gas alerts us to a gas leak
and tells us to get out of the house.

The smell of gasoline alerts us to a gasoline leak
and tells us to get out of the car.
The burning smell alerts us to fire
and tells us to look around for fire.
The burning smell alerts the housewife
that she forgot the pan on the burning stove.
The burning smell in the powder room
tells that the hair drier is not turned off.
An unpleasant body odor alerts the person
that it is time to take a bath with soap.
An unpleasant smell from the mouth
could tell us that the person has gum disease
or a gastrointestinal illness.
An abnormal smell of urine could tell us that
the person has a bladder infection
and should go and see a doctor.
The smell of poop from a baby
warns the mother to change the diaper.
The smell of urine and poop in hallways
of nursing homes tells the hygiene inspectors
that the residents' hygiene is not being taken care of.
The smell of garbage tells us
that the area is unhygienic.

We smell food to know if it is rotten.
We smell food to know if it is cooked well.
We smell mangoes to know if they are ripe or not.
We smell jackfruits to know if they are ripe or not.
We smell food before we eat it.
We smell drinks to find out what drink it is.
We smell the spice in our food.

If we have no sense of smell:
We cannot enjoy the smell of flowers.
We cannot enjoy our meals,
as the aroma of the food

makes our meals luscious.
The smell of food reaches us
before we start to eat
and it helps us to enjoy the food.
When we walk into a house for a party
and are at the entrance of the house,
the aroma of the food tells us
what the host has prepared for us.

Smell awakens our emotions,
as it is connected to the limbic system.
It wakes up our memory.
It controls our behavior and moods too.

Every human being has a unique smell
and it is as good as a fingerprint.
Some like some odors
and some dislike some odors.
We subconsciously pick partners
based on the smell that we like,
giving us good biological matches
and lifelong relationships.
Smell helps us to like our partners.

We all like various fragrances.
Fragrance evokes emotions.
If people did not like fragrances
the whole fragrance industry
would be nonexistent.

Gratitude is the mother of virtues.
If there is no mother, there are no children.
Ingratitude is a vice, as gratitude is a virtue.
Ingratitude toward God or man in any form is a vice.
Ingratitude toward God is called irreligion.
Ingratitude entails dereliction of duty.

Ingratitude entails unpaid debt.
Ingratitude entails covert injustice.
Ingratitude entails obliquity.
Ingratitude entails narcissism,
which eventually hurls one into dire desolation.
Let me not be ungrateful!

What can I return to you, my Lord and my God,
for giving me the sense of smell,
so ingeniously designed to aid us
in our mundane life down here on earth?

Turn away your eyes from my sins
of breaking thy commandments:
the first and the third by not acknowledging
the wonderful gift of smell which
you freely gave me out of divine charity,
the fifth by intemperate consumption of food,
the seventh by wasting food by eating too much,
both of which are due to the tempting aromas of the food,
the sixth and the ninth by seducing others
by excessive use of artificial fragrances,
crossing the borders of modesty.

Grant me the grace to thank you
when I like the flavor of the meals.
Grant me the grace not to become a glutton
due to the enticing smell of food.
Grant me the grace to thank you
when I enjoy the smell of flowers.
Grant me the grace to thank you
when I am saved by my sense of smell from various dangers.
Grant me the grace to thank you for making life
more colorful with the sense of smell.
Grant me the grace not to seduce using fragrances.
Grant me the grace not to be a walking perfumery

by spraying perfumes on hairbrushes,
combs, wardrobes, and lingerie dressers.
Grant me the grace not to be immodest
by beckoning others with seductive scents.

What thanks can I offer you, my Lord and my God,
for giving me the wonderful gift of smell
as a boon out of your love and mercy?
I will laud your name, my Lord and my God,
I will chant and applaud your name forever.

9

Talents: The Special Gifts from God

Talents are natural, innate aptitudes.
They are the natural faculties of some
who have the gift or knack
for doing something in a special way.
Talent is a God-given, innate physical
or mental aptitude to do something with flair.
Just as everybody has concupiscence,
everybody has some kind of talent.
The difference is that concupiscence is an extrovert

and will jump onto the stage without being asked to,
but talent is an introvert which needs coaxing and
practice and even some pushing to put her on stage.

Life is made colorful by the talents of people.
All of us enjoy many forms of talents.
We enjoy arts and entertainment:
such as concerts, music, dance, gymnastics,
athletics, field games, movies, novels, stories,
poems, paintings, sculpture, architecture,
paintings, drawings, and the list goes on.
Talents have been given to some people so that
the glory of God can be seen through them.
They can be developed and used for the benefit
of all the peoples on earth by making their
lives more colorful and enjoyable.

When we enjoy music, do we adore the singer,
or thank God for giving the singer the talent?
When we enjoy music, do we adore the composer,
or thank God for giving the composer the talent?
When we enjoy music, do we adore the lyricist,
or thank God for giving the lyricist the talent?
When we enjoy a dance, do we adore the dancer,
or thank God for giving the dancer the talent?
When we enjoy a dance, do we adore the choreographer
or thank God for giving the choreographer the talent?
When we enjoy a dance, do we adore the musician,
or thank God for giving the musician the talent?
When we enjoy gymnastics, do we adore the gymnast,
or thank God for giving the gymnast the talent, resilience,
and perseverance to accomplish their athletic feats?
When we enjoy games, do we adore the players,
or thank God for giving them the talent, resilience,
and perseverance to accomplish their athletic feats?
When we see the movies, do we adore the actors,

or thank God for giving them their talent?
When we enjoy reading novels, stories, or poems,
do we adore the writers who wrote them,
or thank God for giving them the talent to do so?
When we admire a painting or sculpture or drawing,
do we adore the painter, sculptor, or artist,
or do we thank God for giving them their talent?

So, the various talents are God-given
and are not due to the merits of the artists,
but it goes without saying that those upon whom
God has showered various talents
must also work hard and improve their talents
and should not sleep on their talents
as the servant who dug a hole in the ground
and hid the coin that his master gave him.

Gratitude is the mother of virtues.
If there is no mother, there are no children.
Ingratitude is a vice, as gratitude is a virtue.
Ingratitude toward God or man in any form is a vice.
Ingratitude toward God is called irreligion.
Ingratitude entails dereliction of duty.
Ingratitude entails unpaid debt.
Ingratitude entails covert injustice.
Ingratitude entails obliquity.
Ingratitude entails narcissism,
which eventually hurls one into dire desolation.
Let me not be ungrateful!

What can I return to you, my Lord and my God,
for showering many with various types of talents
so that their talents proclaim your glory
and make our life on earth enjoyable?

Part I

Turn away your eyes from my sins
of breaking thy commandments:
such as the first and third by idolatry
or replacing you with celebrities
such as movie stars, models, pop singers,
athletes, painters, and sculptors,
and by being lazy about developing God-given talents,
and by not acknowledging the wonderful gifts of talents
which you freely gave me out of divine charity,
and the seventh and the tenth by misusing talents
to amass wealth and fame for oneself instead of sharing
the God-given talents for the good of all people.

Grant me the grace to see your forethought
in showering various kinds of talents upon earth,
so that when we enjoy the fruits of others' talents
we can appreciate how great and wonderful
is your manifold wisdom.
Grant me the grace not to adopt idolatrous practices
by deifying celebrities and models.
Grant me the grace to develop my talents
for the glorification of your name.
Grant me the grace to develop my talents
for the betterment of mankind.
Grant me the grace not to bury my talents
on account of sloth or fear.
Grant me the grace not to steal your place
and instead tell the world
that it is not my merit, but your gift to me.
Grant me the grace to share the fruits of my talents
with everyone else for Your sake.
Grant me the grace not to misuse my talents
by using it to amass wealth and fame for myself.
Grant me the grace not to sell my talents
by bidding it in the open market for the highest quote.
Grant me the grace to use my talents
just to earn my livelihood and share the rest with the world.

Grant me the grace, if I am an educator, to *ex ducere,*
or to draw out, the inborn qualities in my students.
Grant me the grace not to push my child into medicine
when his talent is that of an artist.
Grant me the grace, if I am a singer,
to mentor and develop the talent of another
if he has the innate talent for singing.
Grant me the grace, if I am an actor,
not to pull the rug under another with the talent to act
so that he does not steal my pomp and blare.
Grant me the grace to mentor others
who are gifted with talents similar to mine,
and not to envy them or try to sabotage their efforts
so that they do not steal my niche in the halls of fame.

What thanks can I offer you, my Lord and my God,
for showering many with the priceless gift of talents
as a boon out of your love and mercy?
I will laud your name, my Lord and my God,
I will chant and applaud your name forever.

10

Inventions and Discoveries: The Mother of Necessities

Timeline of historic inventions

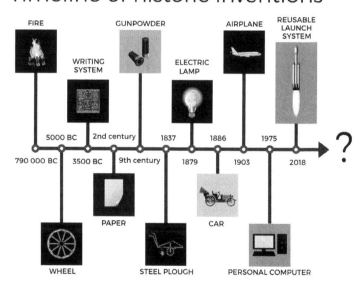

Inventions and discoveries are achieved by creative intelligence, a type of talent given by God to some.

Look at some simple inventions, like the wheel.
Imagine a world without wheels:

then we would have no cars, motorcycles, or buses,
no airplanes, trolleys, or trains,
no cycles or rickshaws,
no chariots or bullock carts,
no skateboards or roller skaters,
no pulleys to draw water from wells,
no motors to pump water to houses and water tanks.

Imagine a life without fire:
then we would not be able to light a candle,
and we would have to eat raw meat and fish,
or raw grains and vegetables,
then there would be no such thing as cooking,
and there would be no heat to drive the cold away.

Imagine a life without electricity:
then there would be no bulbs to see at night,
no heating and air conditioning
no refrigerators, microwaves, or toasters,
no motors or generators,
no trains, planes, or ships.

Imagine a life without printing presses or telephones:
then we would not be able ot talk to those afar
or know what is going around.

Imagine a life without wi-fi or the internet:
then we would not be able to search for information at home,
or shop online anymore.

Imagine a life without currencies or credit cards:
then we would have to exchange cows for grains,
and we would have to use the barter system.

Imagine a life without bricks, steel, or concrete:
then we would have no buildings or houses,
and would have to pitch tents to live in.

Part I

Imagine a life without alphabets, pens, or computers:
then we would not be able to write or draw anything,
would have to add and subtract using our fingers,
would have no written communication
and would have to use old cuneiform.

If Edison or someone else had not invented incandescent lamp:
the night would be pitch dark except for the moon,
there would be no streetlights,
no traffic signals,
no work at night,
no cars or buses at night,
no flights at night,
no cruises at night,
no lighthouses,
hospitals would be dead at night.
At night, the world would come to a standstill.

Forget about the great inventions of Edison.
Open your eyes and look at yourself!
Look at your shirt:
Somebody invented the farming of cotton.
Somebody invented the harvesting of cotton.
Somebody invented ginning.
Somebody invented weaving.
Somebody invented the loom for the cloth.
Somebody invented how to make the fabric.
Somebody invented the design of the shirt.
Somebody invented the cutting.
Somebody invented the machine to stitch it.
Somebody invented the needle for it.
Somebody invented its collar.
Somebody invented the buttons and the holes.
Somebody invented the placket.
Somebody invented the sleeve and the cuff,
and somebody invented the bottom seam.

Look at your pants:
Somebody invented the pants you wear.
Somebody invented the zips.
Somebody invented the waistband.
Somebody invented the belt loops.
Somebody invented the belt and buckles.
Somebody invented the pockets.
Somebody invented the zipper fly.
and somebody invented the bottom hem.

Look at your shoes:
Somebody invented the shoes you wear.
Somebody invented rubber tapping.
Somebody invented the rubber it is made of.
Somebody invented the vulcanization of rubber.
Somebody invented the mold for it.
Somebody invented the toe cap and toe vamp.
Somebody invented the tongue.
Somebody invented the eye stay, eyelets, and lace.
Somebody invented the collar and heel tab.
Somebody invented midsole, outsole, and heel.
You are wearing the fruits of many inventions
of many unknown and immortal inventors.

Am I thankful to anyone for my shirt?
Am I thankful to anyone for my pants?
Am I thankful to anyone for my shoes?
Am I thankful to anyone that I am clad?
Or do I say, "I purchased it, it is mine?"
If so, what have I invented for mankind
and what have I contributed to mankind
which they can purchase with their money?

Gratitude is the mother of virtues.
If there is no mother, there are no children.
Ingratitude is a vice, as gratitude is a virtue.

Part I

Ingratitude toward God or man in any form is a vice.
Ingratitude toward God is called irreligion.
Ingratitude entails dereliction of duty.
Ingratitude entails unpaid debt.
Ingratitude entails covert injustice.
Ingratitude entails obliquity.
Ingratitude entails narcissism,
which eventually hurls one into dire desolation.
Let me not be ungrateful!

What can I return to you, my Lord and my God,
for showering creative talents on many a person,
whose myriad inventions and discoveries
make life tolerable, easier, and enjoyable?

Turn away your eyes from my sins
of breaking thy commandments:
such as the first by placing celebrities in your niche
and the third by not acknowledging the wonderful
gifts of talents for discovery and inventions
which you freely gave me out of divine charity,
the seventh by fostering individualism,
and by selling inventions at unjust prices,
and the tenth by usurping talents by greed.

Grant me the grace to see your hands
behind all inventions and discoveries,
as the source of their talents and drive
were mechanized by your providence.
Grant me the grace to support those with talents
so they might develop their talents for the good of all.
Grant me the grace to sponsor a gifted student
if he does not have the means to go to school.
Grant me the grace to sponsor an inventor
if he does not have the means to do the research.
Grant me the grace not to replace you with

celebrities, inventors, and discoverers.
Grant me the grace not to sell my talents
just for monetary benefits in marketplaces.
Grant me the grace to find medicines to cure diseases,
but not to charge exorbitant prices for them,
under the pretext of research and development costs,
to the detriment of people who cannot make both ends meet.
Grant me the grace to share the fruits of my talents with others,
free of outrageous charges, as you gave them to me for free.

What thanks can I offer you, my Lord and my God,
for showering many with creative intelligence
as a boon out of your love and mercy?
I will laud your name, my Lord and my God,
I will chant and applaud your name forever.

11

The Unique Self: The Image and Likeness of God

Who am I?
What am I?
Where am I?
Am I really alive, or is my life a dreary dream?
Or is my life a sweet dream of a cozy life on earth,
dreamt by an unknown angel in heaven
who will one day wake up
and find, to his solace, with a sigh,

that life on earth was just a dream?
Or am I really alive because of *cogito ergo sum,*
which means, "I think, therefore, I am?"
Whatever it be, for the time being
let me believe that I am really alive on this earth
and I am a unique person with my own identity.

What is the yardstick of my personal identity,
or *identitas,* in Latin, which means "sameness?"
Is it the continuance of bodily existence?
But my body is not always the same,
as all the cells in my body, except brain cells,
are replaced many times during my life.
Is it the continuance of consciousness?
But I am not conscious when I go to sleep,
and so it breaks the continuity of consciousness.
Is it the continuance of my memory?
But if I lose my memory due to a head injury
then am I going to be a different person?
Or as I cannot remember myself
from the first three or four years of my life
how can I be sure I am the same person?
Is it the recollection of past life experiences?
But if I forget some of my past experiences,
am I going to be a different person?
Is it consciousness itself, with no link to body?
Or is it consciousness, with some link to body?
Or is it the intricate and indescribable qualia?
Or is it something else?

I enjoy my life in different ways:
When I enjoy a melodious song,
who is enjoying the song: I, or my ears?
When I enjoy a luscious meal,
who is enjoying the meal: I or my tongue?
When I enjoy the beauty of nature,

who is enjoying it: I or my eyes?
When I enjoy a drawing or a painting
who is enjoying it: I or my eyes?
When I enjoy smelling a rose,
who is enjoying it: I or my nose?
When I like somebody,
what is liking that person: My eyes or my mind?
When I enjoy a novel,
who is enjoying it: I or my brain?
When I love somebody,
who is loving them: I or my brain?
When I walk,
who is walking: I or my legs?
When I swing my hands,
who is swinging them: I or my hands?

When I am in mental anguish,
or in physical pain,
who is in anguish or pain?
Is it my heart, or is it my brain,
or is it my body or is it my soul?

They say there is no soul:
They say everything is in the brain.
They say everything is in neurons.
They say the brain controls everything.
When I am dead my brain is there,
not a small piece is missing from it.
If I am my brain, then why am I dead?
They say the brain cells died
because of lack of blood.
Why was there a lack of blood?
They say the heart stopped working.
If the brain controls everything,
who told the heart to stop working?
The brain will not tell the heart not to work;

that is suicidal.
Then the heart must be more important than brain,
but they say the heart obeys the brain,
but the brain is dead because the heart stopped.
So, the brain is not the master.
The master is neither the brain nor the heart.

It is what I call my soul.
The soul is the subsistent form of life.
My body is evolved, but not my soul.
Soul is the form of my body
and my body is in my soul.
Form is not for matter
but matter is for form.
Soul is the life of my body.
When the soul leaves the body
the heart stops and the brain dies.
The body dies when the soul forsakes it.
Then my soul exists, but not my body.
I am not my body,
and I am not my soul either,
I am the union of soul and body
and I become myself in resurrection.

Man was created in the image and likeness of God.
Just as God has dominion over the universe,
man has dominion over everything on earth.
Just as God has spiritual and moral attributes,
man has natural, spiritual, and moral attributes,
even though he lost some morality at the fall of Adam.
Just as God has free will, man has free will.
Just as God can do whatever he wills to do,
man has free will to do whatever he wants to do.
If God is eternal, man is aeviternal.
Just as God is a thinking thought where
the thinker is God the Father,

the thought is God the Son,
and the relationship between the thinker
and the thought is the Holy Spirit,
man has the ability for introspection,
where the thinker is man, the object of thought is self,
and the bonding of the two is the soul.
Unlike all other creations of God
man has the capacity to know and love God.
Man is endowed with the moral, spiritual, and intellectual
nature of God to mirror his divinity on earth.
Even though man is an imperfect image of God,
man is the divine representation of God on earth,
and so has the duty to live up to God's image and likeness.
I, being a man, must manifest
God's image and likeness down here on earth,
and must see him in all other human beings on earth.

Should I not be grateful to God
for creating my unique self,
comprised of body and soul,
with no other replica of myself
in the whole vast universe,
in all the ages of the world,
to manifest his image and likeness down on earth
and to know and love Him, my Creator,
and to be with Him in His kingdom forever and ever?

Gratitude is the mother of virtues.
If there is no mother, there are no children.
Ingratitude is a vice, as gratitude is a virtue.
Ingratitude toward God or man in any form is a vice.
Ingratitude toward God is called irreligion.
Ingratitude entails dereliction of duty.
Ingratitude entails unpaid debt.
Ingratitude entails covert injustice.
Ingratitude entails obliquity.

Ingratitude entails narcissism,
which eventually hurls one into dire desolation.
Let me not be ungrateful!

What can I return to you, my Lord and my God,
for creating me as a unique person in the world,
not as a remnant of yourself, but as a whole being
in your own image and likeness?

Turn away your eyes from my sins
of breaking thy commandments:
the first and the third by my ingratitude
of not acknowledging your mercy
of creating me in your own image and likeness,
to be with you in your celestial abode forever,
and by breaking all other eight commandments
by not manifesting your image and likeness
to those around me,
and by not seeing your image and likeness
in all those around me.

Grant me the grace to believe that I am not my body.
Grant me the grace to believe that I am not my soul.
Grant me the grace to believe that I am unique,
with none like me for all time.
Grant me the grace to thank you
for creating me in your image and likeness.
Grant me the grace to discern that
the image of God is in my reason and will
as I can know and love God, my Creator.
Grant me the grace to discern that the likeness
of the soul is its undecaying spiritual state
and its mirroring of God's moral qualities.
Grant me the grace to understand that
I was born not by chance, but by your will.
Grant me the grace not to mar your image

within me upon the face of earth.
Grant me the grace to show your image
to all the peoples on earth.
Grant me the grace to see your image
when I look at others here on earth.

What thanks can I offer you, my Lord and my God,
for creating me in your own image and likeness
to share your celestial life forever
as a boon out of your love and mercy?
I will laud your name, my Lord and my God,
I will chant and applaud your name forever.

Part II

"You spring forth fountains in steep valleys.
The waters will cross through the midst of the mountains.
All the wild beasts of the field will drink. The wild
donkeys will anticipate in their thirst. Above them,
the flying things of the air will dwell. From the midst of the
rocks, they will utter voices. You irrigate the
mountains from your heights. The earth will be satiated from
the fruit of your works, producing grass for cattle
and herbs for the service of men. So may you draw bread
from the earth, and wine, in order to cheer the heart
of man. Then he may gladden his face with oil, and bread
will confirm the heart of man."[1]

---

1. Ps 103:10–15 (CPDV).

12

The Earth: The Pond of the Science-Frog

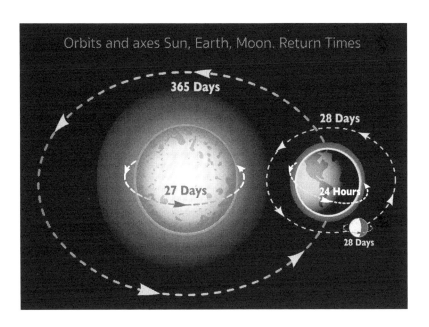

My house sits on the lap of a hillock
nestled in the labyrinth of streams and rivulets
on the planet called Earth,
which revolves around the Sun,
a medium star in the Milky Way galaxy,
which contains billions of stars.

Part II

This giant Milky Way is just one galaxy,
belonging to a local cluster of galaxies,
belonging to a super-galaxy cluster,
containing hundreds of local clusters,
measuring millions of light years in diameter,
and the universe consists of millions
of such super-clusters, with no horizon
to limit its size as we know of it now,
which tells me that Earth can be compared
to a nanodroplet of water that makes up the
the vast oceans of the whole earth.

The earth rotates from west to east
causing the sun to rise in the east and set in the west.
What if the earth rotated from north to south,
showing the same face to the sun?
Then one side of the earth would be facing the sun
for all eternity and would be fiery hot
and it would be day on that side for eternity
and that side would not have been inhabitable.
What about the other side which is away from the sun?
It would be icy frozen as there is no heat from the sun,
and it would be night there for all eternity,
making that side too uninhabitable to humans or animals.
So, the earth is designed to rotate from west to east,
to make earth inhabitable for living beings.
Is it mere chance or an immaculate and purposeful design?

The earth's rotational axis is tilted
and it revolves around the sun in 365 days,
and so we get the four different seasons,
which makes the life on earth colorful.
What if the axis of earth was not tilted that way?
Then there would have been no seasons.
Is it mere chance or an impeccable and purposeful design?

The Earth: The Pond of the Science-Frog

The earth rotates on its axis
completing one rotation in twenty-four hours.
It gives us twelve hours of day and twelve hours of night,
giving twelve hours to work and twelve hours to sleep,
balancing the rhythm of our mundane life.
What if the earth completed one rotation every 140 years?
Then one day would be 140 years:
the daylight would be for 70 years
and the night would be 70 years too.
If we were born into such a world above
life on earth would not be bearable
and it would not make any sense either,
for one day of such an earth would be 140 years,
seventy years of daylight and seventy years of night.
If the average human life span is seventy years,
then a person would have only half of a day to live,
living all his seventy years in the sunlight
or living all his seventy years in the moonlight
which would make life on earth unbearable.
Is it mere chance or thoughtful and purposeful design?

What if the earth completed one revolution
around the sun in 280 years instead of 365 days?
Then each season would be seventy years.
One who is born in the beginning of summer
would die at the end of summer and all
his life would be spent in hot summer.
One who is born in the beginning of winter
would die at the end of winter and all
his life would be spent in the cold winter snow.
One who is born in the early spring
would die at the end of the spring and all
his life would be spent in the spring.
One who is born at the onset of fall
would die at the end of the fall and all
his life would be spent in the season of fall.

Part II

All must eat only the fruits and grains
that grow in the season in which they are born,
and they can only see the beauty of nature
in the season into which they are born.
Some would spend their whole lives in ice and snow.
Some would spend their whole lives in the arid sun.
Some would never see the flowers bloom.
Some would never see the beauty of fallen leaves.
Some would never go to beaches.
Some would spend their whole lives in torrential rain.
Life would be hard and monotonous for all.
The earth completes one revolution in one year,
and not in 280 years, so that all can bear and enjoy life.
Is it mere chance or ingenious and purposeful design?

What if the earth were a little closer to the Sun?
Then it would be uninhabitable due to excessive heat.
What if the earth were a little farther from the Sun?
Then it would be uninhabitable due to excessive cold.
Is it mere chance or purposeful design?

If we buy a ticket for the lotto and win the grand prize
we call it chance.
If we buy a ticket for the lotto
and win the grand prize ten times in a row
would we call it chance?
Is the current position of earth chance?
Is the fact that it is not closer to the sun chance?
Is the fact that it is not farther from the sun chance?
Is the rotation of earth from west east instead of
north to south or south to north chance?
Is the rotation time of twenty-four hours instead of
any other period chance?
Is the revolution time of 365 days
instead of any other time period chance?
Chance is the occurrence of events without any planning.

If many phenomena happen for a particular end,
i.e., the habitability of humans on earth,
then it is not called chance, it is called purposeful design.

Gratitude is the mother of virtues.
If there is no mother, there are no children.
Ingratitude is a vice, as gratitude is a virtue.
Ingratitude toward God or man in any form is a vice.
Ingratitude toward God is called irreligion.
Ingratitude entails dereliction of duty.
Ingratitude entails unpaid debt.
Ingratitude entails covert injustice.
Ingratitude entails obliquity.
Ingratitude entails narcissism,
which eventually hurls one into dire desolation.
Let me not be ungrateful!

What can I return to you, my Lord and my God,
for creating this wonderful earth the way it is
so that it is inhabitable for all living beings
and also designed to make life enjoyable?

Turn away your eyes from my sins
of breaking thy very first and third commandments
by not acknowledging the meticulous creation of earth,
making it inhabitable for all beings.

Grant me the grace to see your hands, daily,
behind the rising sun on the eastern horizon.
Grant me the grace to see your hands, daily,
behind the setting sun in the western horizon.
Grant me the grace to think of your wisdom
as the seasons roll from one to another.
Grant me the grace to wonder at your design
when days and nights alternate.
Grant me the grace to believe in your providence

Part II

when the earth and all other planets and moons
in the solar system keep their assigned paths,
just as soldiers marching in a ceremonial parade
march without disrupting their columns and files.

What thanks can I offer you, my Lord and my God,
for the ingenious and infallible design of the earth,
making it inhabitable for us from time immemorial!
I will laud your name, my Lord and my God,
I will chant and applaud your name forever.

13

The Precious Water: The Universal Solvent

Life without water is unimaginable on earth:
Water is needed by all to survive.
Without water, humans can survive only
three to four days.
Water is needed by plants to produce oxygen.
Without oxygen, humans cannot survive
for more than three to five minutes.
Water is needed by plants to produce food.

Without food, humans and animals will die.
If animals die, humans get no meat.
Water is needed by human cells
in order to keep their shape and structure.
Water is needed by humans and all animals
as blood is a water-based solution.
It carries all nutrients to the cells
and helps to absorb vitamins and minerals.
Without water, the volume of blood is reduced,
blood pressure goes down, blood thickens,
making it harder for the heart to pump it,
and ultimately the heart may fail.
Water is needed to flush out bodily waste,
to regulate body temperature,
and to lubricate various joints in the body.
But water cannot be stored in the body
and needs to be replenished continuously,
and so, water is vital for all living beings
and humans are no exception.
Water is also needed for washing and bathing.
It washes away all the dirt in the world.

So, after oxygen, water is one of the most precious things
we need to survive on this terrestrial planet.
From whence do we get this most precious and
life-sustaining water for our survival?

Look at the clouds in the sky,
at different heights,
in all imaginable shapes and hues:
the cirrus, stratus, cumulus, and nimbus,
each with alto and strato status in each of them.

The heat of the sun causes water to evaporate
from oceans and rivers and lakes.
The water vapors rise into the wind to higher altitudes,

forming clouds of water droplets
which become different types of clouds.

The low-hanging stratus produces rain.
The high-hanging stratus produces snow.
The cumulonimbus provides heavy rains,
and the dreaded thunderstorms and lightning.
The rain falls in the gullies of mountaintops
forming streams and rivers and lakes,
thus distributing water to all the peoples on earth.
It ultimately reaches the lakes, seas, and oceans,
then it evaporates once again, restarting the cycle.

Who designed this impeccable water cycle?
Whose ingenious brain formulated the idea of
heating the ocean water with solar heat,
moving the vapors with pressure difference
and causing them to form into multifarious clouds,
and set up the lab in the vast open sky to mix
the gases to form water and make it fall on earth
in order to sustain all life on earth,
maintaining the same cycle for eons?

Gratitude is the mother of virtues.
If there is no mother, there are no children.
Ingratitude is a vice, as gratitude is a virtue.
Ingratitude toward God or man in any form is a vice.
Ingratitude toward God is called irreligion.
Ingratitude entails dereliction of duty.
Ingratitude entails unpaid debt.
Ingratitude entails covert injustice.
Ingratitude entails obliquity.
Ingratitude entails narcissism,
which eventually hurls one into dire desolation.
Let me not be ungrateful!

Part II

What can I return to you, my Lord and my God,
for giving me life-sustaining water day after day,
and also for sustaining the unfailing mechanism
of watering the world for eons without any glitch?

Turn away your eyes from my sins:
of breaking thy very first and third commandments
by not acknowledging Your mercy
shown in the giving of life-sustaining water
and for maintaining it for all time,
and of breaking the seventh and the tenth
by not sharing the water you have freely given us
with needy neighbors, states, and countries.

Grant me the grace to see your hands
above the vault of the sky,
pouring water on the good and the bad alike,
watering all the vegetation on earth,
just as a gardener waters his plants.
Grant me the grace to visualize your hands
behind the dark nimbus clouds.
Grant me the grace to see your hands
behind the snow that falls from the sky.
Grant me the grace to see your hands
behind the gullies that flow from mountaintops,
transforming them into streams, rivers, and lakes,
to reach the distant, arid lands,
just as farmers make canals and water channels.
Grant me the grace to share my water
with the parched and thirsty,
whether it is man or beast or bird.
Grant me the grace to share the water in my well
with my needy neighbors.
Grant me the grace to share the water
that flows through the rills in my fields
with the neighboring farmlands.

Grant me the grace to share the water
that flows through the rivers in my state and country
with other needy states and countries.

Grant me the grace to visualize your might
behind the roaring thunder and flashing lightning
arising from your laboratories in the sky,
just as fire and fumes are spit up
from chimneys of industrial factories down on earth.
Grant me the grace to see your wisdom of spurting water
from springs and aquifers underneath.
Grant me the grace to imagine the money
that the world must pay to the supplier everyday
for all the water that falls from the sky.
Grant me the grace not to shrug my shoulders and say,
"I didn't ask for it, it falls free from the sky,
and everyone gets it. Who cares if it rains or not?"

What thanks can I offer you, my Lord and my God,
for giving me water, the life of life,
in never-ending supply, free of charge,
as a boon out of your love and mercy?
I will laud your name, my Lord and my God,
I will chant and applaud your name forever.

14

The Sun: The Propellor of Life on Earth

The sun is the source of all energy and life on earth.
Without the sun there would be no light and heat.
Without heat, the water in oceans, lakes, and rivers

would not evaporate into the atmosphere.
Without evaporation, there would be no clouds,
and without clouds, there would be no rain.
Without rain, there would be no water
for us to drink or to help plants to grow.

Without sun, there would be no heat on earth.
Without heat there would be no winds,
Without winds, air would not move,
and it would not rise, cool, and make rain.
Without winds there would be no ocean currents,
which help maintain the global climate.

Without the sun's heat, earth would be an icy rock.
Without the sun there would be no photosynthesis.
Without photosynthesis there would be no oxygen.
Without oxygen there would be no life on earth.

Without photosynthesis all plants would die.
Without plants there would be no food on earth.
Without food all animals would die.
Without animals and plants, mankind would have no food,
and mankind would die of starvation.

Without the sun there would be no light on earth,
and all would grope around in the dark.
Without the sun there would be no such thing as day.
Without the sun there would be no moonlight
as moonlight is the reflection of light from the sun.
Without moonlight nights would be as pitch as black.

We rely on the sun's energy for many things:
We dry our clothes in the sun.
We dry our grains and corns in the sun.
We make windows so we can
steal the light of the sun from outside.

During the day, we turn the lights off and use sunlight.
We generate electricity using solar panels.
We harness the sun's energy for greenhouses.

We use solar cells for calculators, watches,
and all kinds of electronic appliances.
Without the sun there would be no more solar cells
for watches, calculators, houses, and buildings.
The sunshine also brings us Vitamin D
to help our body absorb calcium in food,
which is needed for body function.

The sun is the source of all life on earth
and it is meticulously designed and placed
to thrive and maintain life on earth.
The sun gives all the energy that is needed
for all beings on Earth,
and the fusion factories installed in the sun
can give incessant energy for billions of years.

The sun is placed at such a meticulous distance
to heat earth's atmosphere to such a degree
as needed for the existence of life on earth.
It is neither boiling hot nor freezing cold.
If it were a little closer, we would die of heat.
If it were a little farther, we would die of cold.

Is the meticulous placement of the sun
mere chance, or ingenious, purposeful design?

Gratitude is the mother of virtues.
If there is no mother, there are no children.
Ingratitude is a vice, as gratitude is a virtue.
Ingratitude toward God or man in any form is a vice.
Ingratitude toward God is called irreligion.
Ingratitude entails dereliction of duty.

Ingratitude entails unpaid debt.
Ingratitude entails covert injustice.
Ingratitude entails obliquity.
Ingratitude entails narcissism,
which eventually hurls one into dire desolation.
Let me not be ungrateful!

What can I return to you, my Lord and my God,
for creating the wonderful sun
and placing it at such a distance from the earth
so as to make the earth inhabitable?

Turn away your eyes from my sins
of breaking thy very first and third commandments
by not acknowledging the creation of
the sun with meticulous care
so that the earth is an inhabitable place.

Grant me the grace to thank you
when I see the sun rise in the east.
Grant me the grace to wonder at your design
when I see the sun traverse the sky over my head.
Grant me the grace to be thankful to you
when I enjoy the beauty of the sunset in the west.
Grant me the grace to thank you for the sunlight
when I see the world through the light of the sun.
Grant me the grace to be thankful for the heat of the sun
when it drives away the frigid coldness.
Grant me the grace to thank you for the free sunshine
when I lay on beaches and bask in the sun.
Grant me the grace to gaze at the moon,
with a heart filled with thanks,
when I walk at night in the moonlight.
Grant me the grace to revere you with gratitude
when I see all forms of life on earth.
Grant me the grace to calculate in my mind

the astronomical amount of money I would owe you
if I ever had to pay for all the sun's light I have used
throughout the entirety of my life.
Grant me the grace not to shrug my shoulders and say,
"I didn't ask for it, it comes free from the sky,
and everyone gets it. Who cares if there is no sun?"

What thanks can I offer you, my Lord and my God,
for the ingenious design of the sun,
and for sustaining it by your providence
as a never-ending source of energy for us?
I will laud your name, my Lord and my God,
I will chant and applaud your name forever.

15

The Wind: The Sun's Winnow

The wind spreads the sun's heat in the atmosphere
and makes the earth inhabitable for all beings.
It moves the ocean currents, regulating global temperature.
It brings to the land rains and storms that form in oceans.
It moves the clouds around and gives us snow and rain.
It brings us the cool breeze from the oceans.
It carries air pollution away from us.

Part II

It helps plants by carrying their seeds far
so that they spring up in distant lands.

It helps sailors at sea
by blowing on the unfurled sails of their boats.
It turns the wind turbines that give us electricity.
It helps us to mill grains with wind power.
It helps us to irrigate farms by pumping water.
It helps us to bear the sun's heat by cooling us,
by slowly evaporating the toil's sweat from us.
It helps bring enjoyment to children as they fly kites,
and helps adults to kitesurf and windsurf.
It helps birds to migrate easily.
The winds make the runways shorter
by helping the planes take off with the winds
and letting them land against them,
saving us construction and maintenance cost.
It helps ejected pilots and paratroopers land safely on ground
without being killed by the fall.
It helps us to dry our clothes without a drier.
The wind blows down ripe mangoes from trees,
saving us from having to climb them.

Whose idea was it to create such an unseen force,
whose presence we only know by its effects
such as the movement of the clouds in the sky,
or the roaring waves along the ocean beaches,
or the much-dreaded thunderstorms and hurricanes,
or the gentle versions of the wind, the breezes,
which rustle leaves, hug and cool us as they pass?

Gratitude is the mother of virtues.
If there is no mother, there are no children.
Ingratitude is a vice, as gratitude is a virtue.
Ingratitude toward God or man in any form is a vice.
Ingratitude toward God is called irreligion.

Ingratitude entails dereliction of duty.
Ingratitude entails unpaid debt.
Ingratitude entails covert injustice.
Ingratitude entails obliquity.
Ingratitude entails narcissism,
which eventually hurls one into dire desolation.
Let me not be ungrateful!

What can I return to you, my Lord and my God,
for creating the mighty winds and the gentle breezes
each with its own specific job to do,
to sustain life on this wonderful planet?

Turn away your eyes from my sins
of breaking thy very first and third commandments
by not acknowledging the creation of winds.

Grant me the grace to thank you for your care,
when I see the moving clouds and falling rains.
Grant me the grace to see your breath
behind the turning windmill blades.
Grant me the grace to feel your hands
when a breeze cools me off.
Grant me the grace to think of your might
when I see vast clouds moving in the sky.
Grant me the grace to thank you for your help
when I see my washed clothes drying in the wind.
Grant me the grace to wonder at your design
when I see the peaking and spilling waves on beaches.
Grant me the grace to ponder on your providence
when I see plants and trees dancing in the wind.
Grant me the grace to thank you for the wind
when my plane takes off safely without overrunning the runway.
Grant me the grace to thank you for the wind
when my plane lands safely without overshooting the runway.
Grant me the grace to thank you for this unseen force

without which life on earth would have been a dream.
Grant me the grace not to shrug my shoulders and say,
I didn't ask for winds, it comes from somewhere
and goes somewhere. Who cares for the wind?

What thanks can I offer you, my Lord and my God,
for creating the precious and invisible wind
as a boon out of your mercy and care?
I will laud your name, my Lord and my God,
I will chant and applaud your name forever.

1 6

The Atmosphere: The Fortification of Earth

Layers of Earth's Atmosphere

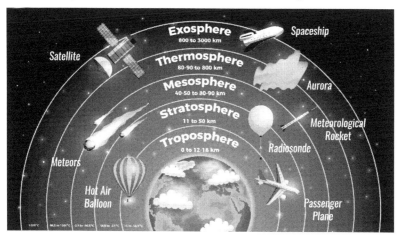

The earth has 300 miles of atmosphere
consisting of five layers:
the troposphere, stratosphere, mesosphere,
thermosphere, and exosphere.

What if there was no troposphere
covering the first ten miles from the ground?
Then there would be no oxygen

for us to breath, and no rain or wind or snow,
as all these are formed in this vital layer.
There would be no living beings on earth
if the troposphere did not contain what it contains.
Its role is to hold enough air for photosynthesis
so that trees and plants can make enough oxygen
for us and animals to breath, and to make food
for plants themselves and all living beings on earth.

What if there was no stratosphere
for the fifteen miles after that?
This is where the ozone is formed
by the bonding of oxygen atoms.
The ozone layer shields the earth
from the sun's injurious ultraviolet radiation.
Without the ozone layer, life would be miserable.

What if there was no mesosphere
for the twenty-five miles beyond that,
acting as a meteor shield for our earth?
If it were not there, then meteors,
or shooting stars as we call them,
would bombard our earth, making craters and turbulence
upon the face of the earth, making it uninhabitable.
For it is in this sphere that all the meteors
are burnt out as they continue their downward
flight to the earth from outer space.

What if there was no thermosphere
that extends another 250 miles or so?
It is here where the space stations orbit.
This sphere is the cradle of communications,
without which there would not be the kind of
intercontinental communications we have today.

What if there was no exosphere beyond that?
It is the protector of all the layers below it,
absorbing radioactive rays from the sun
and housing communications satellites.

All these different layers of atmosphere,
each with its own job to do,
make life feasible on earth,
and make earth inhabitable to us humans.
Is this multilayered atmospheric system,
each layer with specific duties to perform,
mere chance or design?
Are we blind to see the purposeful design
of each layer, with its own specific job,
to attain the common goal of habitability on earth?

Gratitude is the mother of virtues.
If there is no mother, there are no children.
Ingratitude is a vice, as gratitude is a virtue.
Ingratitude toward God or man in any form is a vice.
Ingratitude toward God is called irreligion.
Ingratitude entails dereliction of duty.
Ingratitude entails unpaid debt.
Ingratitude entails covert injustice.
Ingratitude entails obliquity.
Ingratitude entails narcissism,
which eventually hurls one into dire desolation.
Let me not be ungrateful!

What can I return you, my Lord and my God,
for creating the multilayered atmosphere,
each layer with its own specific role to play
to make earth inhabitable for us on earth?

Turn away your eyes from my sins
of breaking thy very first and third commandments

by not acknowledging the creation of
the multilayered atmosphere to ensure
that the earth is inhabitable for humans.

Grant me the grace to thank your wisdom
when I breath in the oxygen manufactured
in the green laboratories of the troposphere.
Grant me the grace to thank you for your care
when I enjoy the products of the troposphere,
such as the wind, the rain, the snow,
and everything else that sprouts from them.
Grant me the grace to thank you for the ozone layer
which protects me from ultraviolet radiation.
Grant me the grace to thank you for your wisdom
when I use my cell phone,
supported by satellites in the thermosphere and exosphere.
Grant me the grace to think of your wisdom
when I see shooting stars falling
and burning in the mesosphere
thus not falling on my head and killing me.
Grant me the grace to thank you for the multilayered
atmosphere which makes life possible on earth.
Grant me the grace not to shrug my shoulders and say,
I didn't ask for the layers, it is how things are here,
who cares about these layers?

What thanks can I offer you, my Lord and my God,
for the ingenious design of the various
layers of the atmosphere for my
sustenance, subsistence, and protection?
I will laud your name, my Lord and my God,
I will chant and applaud your name forever.

17

Photosynthesis: The Scaffold of Life

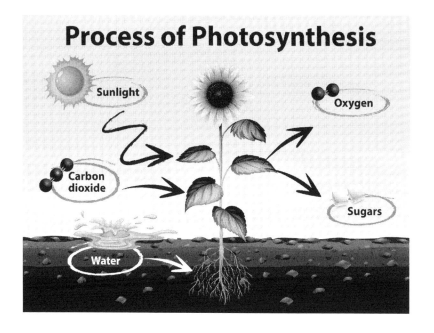

What is photosynthesis?
It is the transfer of light energy into chemical energy.
Plants have leaves which contain chlorophyll.
The chlorophyll captures sunlight,
and using carbon dioxide in the atmosphere,
and water and minerals in the ground,

it converts light energy into carbohydrates
and gives away oxygen as a byproduct,
making food for the whole world
and oxygen for all to breathe.

If there were no such thing as photosynthesis,
there would be no plants,
and if there were no plants,
there would be no grains or fruits,
and if there were no grains or fruits,
there would be nothing for living beings to eat,
and all the animals would die of starvation,
so there would be no cows or goats to give us milk
and there would be no hens or ducks to give us eggs.

All the animals which give us meat for food
are herbivorous and the plants they eat
are transformed into meat in their own body.
If there were no plants for animals to eat,
they would not be able to produce any meat.

If there were no grains or vegetables to eat
and if there were no meat to eat
then there would be no food for mankind
and all humans would die of starvation,
for the fuel of the food bank is photosynthesis.

The oxygen needed for living organisms
come from plants during photosynthesis:
If there were no plants,
there would be no photosynthesis,
if there were no photosynthesis,
then there would be no oxygen,
and if there were no oxygen,
no man or beast can live,
so, the scaffold of our life is photosynthesis.

Are we blind to see the thoughtful design
of photosynthesis to sustain life on earth?
Who has the patent for the invention of photosynthesis?
Who has the secret code to the combination
of making oxygen and food from photosynthesis?

Gratitude is the mother of virtues.
If there is no mother, there are no children.
Ingratitude is a vice, as gratitude is a virtue.
Ingratitude toward God or man in any form is a vice.
Ingratitude toward God is called irreligion.
Ingratitude entails dereliction of duty.
Ingratitude entails unpaid debt.
Ingratitude entails covert injustice.
Ingratitude entails obliquity.
Ingratitude entails narcissism,
which eventually hurls one into dire desolation.
Let me not be ungrateful!

What can I return to you, my Lord and my God,
for sustaining life on earth with photosynthesis,
the ingenious process of converting light energy
into various forms of energy to sustain life on earth?

Turn away your eyes from my sins:
of breaking thy very first and third commandments
by not acknowledging your mercy seen through
energizing the earth with photosynthesis,
and for maintaining it for endless years,
and also for breaking the seventh by not
taking care of plants and trees.

Grant me the grace to see your hands
in all the plants and trees I see.
Grant me the grace to see your wisdom
in each breath of oxygen I breathe.

Part II

Grant me the grace to thank you for your wisdom
when I enjoy the shade of a tree.
Grant me the grace to see your providence
in trees, steppes, and forests.
Grant me the grace to be thankful to you
for your gift in the form of photosynthesis.

What thanks can I offer you, my Lord and my God,
for all the plants, forests, and trees,
and the life-sustaining process of photosynthesis
which you have designed thoughtfully
as a boon out of your love and mercy?
I will laud your name, my Lord and my God,
I will chant and applaud your name forever.

18

Oxygen: The Soul of Life

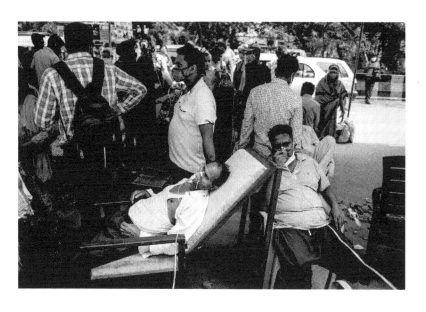

Oxygen is the soul of life, without which
none can survive upon the face of the globe.
If deprived of oxygen for five minutes:
the brain cells and the heart cells die.
If the heart stops, respiration stops,
and if respiration stops, more brain cells die,
then other body cells do not get oxygen-rich blood
and they also start dying, one by one.

None on earth can survive without oxygen.
Every tissue and cell needs oxygen.
Humans need hundreds of liters of pure oxygen per day.
Do we pay for it, or is it a free boon from above?
If you want to know the value of the oxygen you breathe daily,
contract COVID-19 and get admitted into a hospital
and be on a ventilator for twenty-four hours.
They will charge you at least
ten thousand dollars for giving you oxygen
for twenty-four hours, and you cannot
live for more than a couple of days
if you have to buy oxygen from them
at that unaffordable price.
Think of all those who have died in hospitals,
at homes, and on the streets, gasping for oxygen
due to the dire shortage of oxygen in some countries
during the COVID-19 pandemic.

In addition to the oxygen we need for daily life,
we need extra oxygen for many diseases,
such as COPD, emphysema, lung cancer,
asthma, COVID-19, pleural effusion, seizures,
heart failure, pneumonia, cystic fibrosis,
sleep apnea, bronchitis, surgeries, and the like.

What is the source of this life-sustaining oxygen?
We get it from the air we breathe in,
which contains about twenty percent oxygen.
Whence does the air get the oxygen?
Seventy-five percent of the oxygen in the air
comes from ocean plants that live near the ocean surface,
and the rest is a byproduct of photosynthesis,
of marine and terrestrial biosphere
and silica minerals from the lithosphere.
It is also produced by trees, which absorb carbon dioxide

from the atmosphere and water from the ground,
in the presence of sunlight,
making oxygen through the process of photosynthesis.

If we were to purchase all the oxygen
we would need for an entire lifetime,
then it would cost an unaffordable sum of money,
and all the money we make would be insufficient
to ensure our survival here.
When we get this oxygen free from the air,
do we ever thank the ecosystems, the marine plants,
or the trees for providing this precious gas to us for free?
Or do we thank the Great Scientist
who mechanized the whole ecosystem
to produce this most-wanted oxygen,
the sine qua non of life of all living creatures on earth?

The earth is a closed system,
nothing comes in and nothing goes out.
Who designed the great formulae
to generate the never-failing oxygen supply
in the great laboratories of the biosphere?
Who programmed the marine and terrestrial biosphere
to absorb water and carbon dioxide from around
and mix it with sunshine to produce the oxygen
which is much needed for our existence?

Gratitude is the mother of virtues.
If there is no mother, there are no children.
Ingratitude is a vice, as gratitude is a virtue.
Ingratitude toward God or man in any form is a vice.
Ingratitude toward God is called irreligion.
Ingratitude entails dereliction of duty.
Ingratitude entails unpaid debt.
Ingratitude entails covert injustice.

Part II

Ingratitude entails obliquity.
Ingratitude entails narcissism,
which eventually hurls one into dire desolation.
Let me not be ungrateful!

What can I return to you, my Lord and my God,
for giving me life-sustaining oxygen as a boon,
delivering it free of charge to the consumption point,
right into my nose, unfailingly, without any shortage?

Turn away your eyes from my sins,
of breaking thy very first and third commandments,
by not acknowledging your mercy
of giving us much-needed oxygen as a gift from above.

Grant me the grace to thank the Mighty Designer
for providing the never-ending oxygen supply.
Grant me the grace to see the hands of the Great Chemist
behind the never-ending supply of oxygen.
Grant me the grace not to destroy his laboratories
by cutting down the trees in the biosphere.
Grant me the grace to help his laboratory
by planting trees, shrubs, and bushes around my house.
Grant me the grace to thank you at least once in a while
when I inhale the much-needed oxygen in the air.
Grant me the grace to remember that the oxygen
in every breath of mine is a gift from you.
Grant me the grace not to consider oxygen worthless
as I receive it freely.
Grant me the grace not to shrug my shoulders and say,
I did not ask for it, it is already in the air.
Everybody is breathing it, and I am just one of them.
Why should I be thankful, when nobody is?

What thanks can I offer you, my Lord and my God,
for giving me oxygen, the soul of life,

in never-ending supply, free of charge
as a boon out of your love and mercy?
I will laud your name, my Lord and my God,
I will chant and applaud your name forever.

19

The Staple Foods: The Fuel of the Body

All creatures need food to survive,
be it man or beast or bird.
If there is no food intake
humans will die in three to four weeks.
After oxygen and water,
food is the third-greatest necessity for survival.

Cars cannot run without gas.
Electric bulbs cannot burn without electricity.
Motors cannot run without electricity.
Oil lamps cannot burn without wicks and oil.

The Staple Foods: The Fuel of the Body

Candles cannot burn without wicks and wax.
Humans cannot live without food.

There are thousands of edible plants,
such as rice, wheat, oats, maize, and barley.
Ten to fifteen of these plants make
ninety percent of all our food intake.
Rice, corn, and wheat comprise sixty percent
of all major staple food that is consumed.
Let us look at one of them: the rice plant.

It is the source of energy for billions of people,
and it is the food that alleviates the world's hunger.
It also is the major supplier
of carbohydrates for the needs of the body.

They grow from tiny grains into grassy plants,
with many heads full of tiny grains,
to such an extent that one tiny grain
produces up to a thousand grains
which turn golden when it is time to reap.

Have you ever stood on the causeway of a paddy field
and wondered at the secret behind its growth?
Above the roots on the ground rises many a stem,
and at the end of stems are panicles or multiheaded seed heads,
with hundreds of grains of rice dancing in the wind.

One tiny grain
multiplied into thousands of grains
to give daily food for mankind.
Each grain has a hull and a brown layer of skin,
and the real rice is the hard core with a lot of starch.
A little grain of seed grows into a grassy plant,
with hundreds and hundreds of grains.
Jesus multiplied loaves of bread long ago.

Now he is doing it again with grains of rice.
From the ground of muddy soil and water
spring up the plant and the retinue of grains.
The grains are entirely different from the soil whence it sprang.
What mechanization is involved
in such a wonderful transformation
of edible grains of rice grains
sprouting from the muddy ground of soil and water?

Who is the Scientist who invented
the formula for this transformation
of mud and water into immaculate grains,
sufficient for almost half of the world?
Whose clever hands were behind this programming?
Whose brain was behind the execution
of multiplying one grain into thousands of grains
from muddy soil and water?
Can any laboratory in the whole world
produce grains from mud and water?
Is it chance or immaculate design?

Gratitude is the mother of virtues.
If there is no mother, there are no children.
Ingratitude is a vice, as gratitude is a virtue.
Ingratitude toward God or man in any form is a vice.
Ingratitude toward God is called irreligion.
Ingratitude entails dereliction of duty.
Ingratitude entails unpaid debt.
Ingratitude entails covert injustice.
Ingratitude entails obliquity.
Ingratitude entails narcissism,
which eventually hurls one into dire desolation.
Let me not be ungrateful!

What can I return to you, my Lord and my God,
for giving me life-sustaining staple foods,

by multiplying one grain into thousands of grains
through the secrets hidden in nature's design?

Turn away your eyes from my sins:
of breaking thy very first and third commandments
by not acknowledging your mercy
through giving us life-sustaining staple foods
and for maintaining this supply for endless years,
and the fifth by eating excessive amounts of food,
which is detrimental to longevity of life,
and the seventh and the tenth by not sharing
the food you have created for all humans,
and the ninth by concupiscence of flesh
by eating food inordinately.

Grant me the grace to see your hands
behind every food we eat.
Grant me the grace to give thanks for your bounty
before every meal I take.
Grant me the grace to give thanks for your bounty
after every meal I take.
Grant me the grace to think of all the farmers
who fill our tables with various kinds of food.
Grant me the grace to see the hundreds of hands
that work to bring the food to the table.
Grant me the grace to share my food
with everybody else in the world.
Grant me the grace not to waste any food
as it is the gift of God and product of sweat.
Grant me the grace not to be a glutton
by eating more than is needed.
Grant me the grace not to waste any food
by ordering more than what can fill my stomach.
Grant me the grace to eat to live
and not to live to eat.

Part II

What thanks can I offer you, my Lord and my God,
for designing food staples in never-ending supply,
free of charge, as a boon out of your love and mercy?
I will laud your name, my Lord and my God,
I will chant and applaud your name forever.

20

The Produce: The Universal Food

Produce consists of fruits and vegetables.
There are thousands of different fruits and vegetables on earth.
Some people cannot survive without vegetables,
for they are vegans and eat nothing but vegetables and fruits.
Some are under-the-ground vegans
and some are over-the-ground vegans
who do not eat potatoes, garlic, or onions,

or anything that grows under the ground,
and some others are fruitarians who eat only fruits and grains.

Now let us look at the kingdom of fruits.
Without fruits many of our bodily systems,
such as the cardiac and the digestive,
would be in peril as they do not function well without fruit.
Pineapples digest food and build bones.
Cherries calm our nervous system.
Grapes relax blood vessels and reduce clots.
Bananas give us energy and motivation.
Oranges keep skin young and fresh.
Apples build resistance against infections.
Mangoes help fight cancer.
Garlic is antibacterial, antiviral, and antiseptic.
Cucumbers hydrate the body.
Spinach regulates heart rate and blood pressure.
Broccoli and cabbage give calcium.

Look at the outer coverings of fruits and grains:
Some fruits, such as oranges, have rinds.
Some fruits, such as apples, have skins.
Some fruits, such as bananas, have peels,
Coconuts have thick husks and hard shells.
Grains have husks and nuts have shells.

Did we ever wonder why all fruits and grains
have a protective covering or shell?
We need not storm our brain
to find the reason for all these things.
When we send letters to others
we put them in an envelope and seal them with glue.
When we send any type of goods to anyone,
we wrap it well to ensure it reaches the destination safely.

Look how coconuts are packed for humans.
Look at the tall coconut trees.
They grow eighty to ninety feet tall.
When coconuts are ripe, they fall to the ground.
When harvesting the coconuts,
they are cut and dropped to the ground.
The coconut has three protective layers:
a hard outer coat, a one-inch-thick husk coat,
and a very hard inner shell,
and the real coconut is inside that shell
so that when it falls from a great height
it just bounces like a ball and rolls to rest.
The bottom line is that coconuts are packed
in such a way that they reach us unbroken,
just as Amazon packs laptops and televisions
in multilayered Styrofoam packings
so that they reach customers without breaking.
Is the packing of coconuts chance or design?

Somebody programmed trees, plants, and vegetation
to pack the produce well,
just as we pack the parcels to ensure they reach human beings
in fine shape and without being plundered or opened
by birds and animals on the land and air.

Look at a mango tree,
so filled with mangoes that we cannot see the leaves.
They are of different sizes, colors, and shapes,
some are green, some yellow, and some red.
The mango tree makes the mangoes
from mud, using soil, water, and sunshine.
How can mango fruits come from such
raw and seemingly useless materials?
What is the secret code for that transformation?
Can any laboratory in the world,
with all its scientists and sages,

make one mango fruit?
Can they make an apple using soil and water?
Or a jackfruit or pear using soil and water?

They never can, because they do not have
the wisdom to decipher nature's secret code
of making fruits from soil, water, and sunshine.
Who is the scientist who invented the formula
for this transformation of soil and water
into the much-needed fruits and vegetables
without which we cannot survive?
It is none but the Almighty God.

Are we blind to the clever hands
behind this wonderful innovation of making
produce for mankind from nothingness
and programming all the packing modes
so that they reach human hands
in undamaged and unbroken condition?

Gratitude is the mother of virtues.
If there is no mother, there are no children.
Ingratitude is a vice, as gratitude is a virtue.
Ingratitude toward God or man in any form is a vice.
Ingratitude toward God is called irreligion.
Ingratitude entails dereliction of duty.
Ingratitude entails unpaid debt.
Ingratitude entails covert injustice.
Ingratitude entails obliquity.
Ingratitude entails narcissism,
which eventually hurls one into dire desolation.
Let me not be ungrateful!

What can I return to you, my Lord and my God,
for giving me much-needed produce,
and for packaging it well enough to reach me undamaged?

The Produce: The Universal Food

Turn away your eyes from my sins:
of breaking thy very first and third commandments
by not acknowledging your mercy
of giving us different types of fruits and vegetables
and for maintaining them for endless years,
and also for breaking the seventh and tenth by
not sharing the food you have created for all humans.

Grant me the grace to see your hands
behind every fruit I eat.
Grant me the grace to see your hands
behind every vegetable I eat.
Grant me the grace to appreciate your packing
when I peel a banana or a plantain.
Grant me the grace to look at a half-peeled banana
and muse on how mud and water are changed
into the fleshy part, containing many nutrients,
and how the peel is designed to keep it intact,
and how the color is changed when it is ripe,
telling me, *Come, eat me, I am ripe for you.*
Grant me the grace to appreciate your packing
when I remove the rind of an orange.
Grant me the grace to comprehend and appreciate
why you did not design apples with coconut shells
and coconuts with apple skins.
Grant me the grace to thank you for your goodness
when I eat luscious mangoes and grapes.
Grant me the grace to think of your care
when I chew and enjoy the juicy fruits.
Grant me the grace to think of the hungry
whenever I fill my stomach.
Grant me the grace not to be insane and say,
I do not care if apples had coconut shells and husk
and coconuts had apple skin.

Part II

What thanks can I offer you, my Lord and my God,
for designing fruits and vegetables
in never-ending supply, free of charge,
as a boon out of your love and mercy?
I will laud your name, my Lord and my God,
I will chant and applaud your name forever.

21

Animals: The *Sine Qua Nons*

Life without animals is unthinkable on earth:
Elephants, horses, camels, and donkeys transport us.
Traversing deserts without camels is unimaginable.
Crossing forests and countryside requires horses.
Horse-drawn vehicles were once common.
Warriors and archers fought on horseback.
Bullocks drew the bullock-carts in the countryside.
Bullocks and oxen help us to till the fields.
Decades ago, they filled the role of farm-tillers.
Oxen were used in copra presses to make oil.

Part II

Elephants were used to transport large logs
from country areas to wheelable roads.

Cows, she-goats, and she-buffalo give us milk:
How will coffee and tea taste without milk?
Without milk, there would be no cheese or yogurt.
Hens and ducks give us much-needed eggs
which fill our plates for breakfast and brunch.

Cows, buffaloes, sheep, and oxen give us leather
which is used to make jackets and wallets.

Oxen, cows, sheep, swine, and the like give us meat
such as beef, bacon, and mutton,
without which our main-course plates would go empty.
Meat contains much-needed protein
and five of the vitamin B complexes
necessary for health and well-being.

Chicken, ducks, and turkey also fill our daily plates.
The roosters crow at dawn, waking up clockless farmers.
The manure of animals makes our field fertile,
making our various crops a hundredfold.

Oxen and pigs give us much-needed heparin,
an anticoagulant that is much needed after surgery,
and pigs give gelatin for drug capsules.

Dogs give us fun and recreation, and provide safety.
They help sniff out contraband at airports.
They help detectives trace culprits, intruders, and robbers.

Rats and rabbits help in biomedical research.
They are the testing sites and scapegoats
of our medications, vaccines, and surgeries.
They are our scouts in the laboratories.

Fish is an important part of our daily food.
It is rich in calcium, phosphorous, and minerals.
It is a great source of protein, iodine,
omega fatty acids, and vitamins,
all of which are needed for maintenance
of many body parts and functions.

The copious supply of fish
that feed mankind from time immemorial
multiplies endlessly in the oceans,
lakes, rivers, streams, and ponds.
Who taught them how to multiply
and maintain their progeny for generations?
The more they are caught and consumed,
the more they reproduce and multiply,
making sure the supply never ends.
Is it chance or purposeful design?

Should I not be grateful to all these animals
who work hard to make my life better?
Some of them live and die for our well-being.
Should I not thank God for his
thoughtful inclusion of these animals
on earth to help us to live well?

Gratitude is the mother of virtues.
If there is no mother, there are no children.
Ingratitude is a vice, as gratitude is a virtue.
Ingratitude toward God or man in any form is a vice.
Ingratitude toward God is called irreligion.
Ingratitude entails dereliction of duty.
Ingratitude entails unpaid debt.
Ingratitude entails covert injustice.
Ingratitude entails obliquity.
Ingratitude entails narcissism,

which eventually hurls one into dire desolation.
Let me not be ungrateful!

What can I return to you, my Lord and my God,
for your thoughtful creation and
sustenance of animal life on earth
to help us to survive and thrive on earth?

Turn away your eyes from my sins:
of breaking thy very first and third commandments
by not acknowledging your mercy
of giving us different types of animals
and for maintaining them for endless years,
and also of breaking the seventh by not respecting and
for not using them for their intended purposes.

Grant me the grace to appreciate the
the diversity of creation for man's good.
Grant me the grace to peek into the depth
of the retinue God has created for man's use.
Grant me the grace to love animals,
which work hard to make our lives better.
Grant me the grace to be thankful for sheep and goats,
for the milk, eggs, and meat they give me.
Grant me the grace to think that
they are our helpers in this world.
Grant me the grace to hug cows and goats
and cuddle hens and chickens.

Grant me the grace not to dress dogs and cats
with fur and leather vests and coats, when
children in third-world countries
do not have an under cloth to wear
to hide their nakedness.
Grant me the grace to love animals
but not to give them the affection

that is due only to human beings.
Grant me the grace not to replace
spouses and children with cats and dogs.
Grant me the grace to give to animals what belongs to animals,
and to man what belongs to man.

Grant me the grace to see your hands
behind the fish in the seas and oceans.
Grant me the grace to see your hands
behind the never-ending supply of fish.
Grant me the grace to understand that
Jesus' multiplication of fish
is continuing today in rivers and seas.

What thanks can I offer you, my Lord and my God,
for all the animals on earth
which you have created and sustained to live with us
as a boon out of your love and mercy?
I will laud your name, my Lord and my God,
I will chant and applaud your name forever.

22

The Ancillary Helpers: The Stagehands

The earth is made livable for humans to survive
by many seemingly futile creatures
which were created by the Mastermind
who created even the sparrows with an intent.

Look at the birds in the sky!
Do we ever wonder what they are doing up there,
or why they should be up there, hovering throughout the sky?

They are the agents of nutrient cycling,
soil aeration, seed sowing, pollination,
forest decomposition, and insect control.
If they were not there,
the earth would be swarming with insects,
plants would not reproduce, thus depriving mankind of food,
and forests would disappear from earth.
How useful are the birds in the sky!

Look at the ubiquitous monkeys!
Ever wonder why they are down here?
They are the farmers of tropical forests.
They disperse seeds of fruits and trees as they eat fruits,
and travel miles and miles, spreading the seeds,
which sprout new trees and plants,
and if not for the monkeys, many forests would have disappeared.
How useful are the monkeys!

Look at the worms that wiggle on the field!
With what disgust we look at them?
They work hard to aerate the soil
and to make channels for providing water
for roots of plants to help them grow.
They are also the garbage disposers of the world
without them our earth would be a big trash yard.
They work hard for us without any reward.
How useful are the worms!

What about wasps and spiders!
We hate both beings.
Wasps fly around us with a buzzing noise,
and we fear their painful stings,
but they are the sentries of gardens and crops,
doing pest control for free.
Spiders are all over the world, from cupboards to caves.
We hate them for their scary looks,

and they bite us too,
but they are our allies,
because they perform insect control.
A world without them would be loathsome
as we would be swarmed with lot of pests.
How useful are the wasps and spiders!

Look at the butterflies!
They flutter all around the world.
Like aimless gnats they fly.
They are a feast to the eyes.
They travel far and wide,
pollinating plants and exterminating pests.
If they did not pollinate plants,
there would be no food for us to eat.
They are the food of many animals and birds.
Without them birds would starve.
So the butterflies are busy doing their job
and not fluttering around doing nothing.
How useful are the butterflies!

Have we ever wondered at the bees
flying from one flower to another?
They are the pollinators of plants and flowers,
without whom plants and flowers would have disappeared forever.
They are also the germinators of many a crop,
without whom the crops would fail,
and mankind would have starved to death by now.
They deserve a salute for working hard for us.
How useful are the bees!

Look at the ants that crawl on the ground!
We are ever annoyed by the ubiquitous ants
that crawl all around in every part of the world,
in the field and in the house and in cupboards
and in floor cracks and window sills?

We kill them when they bite us
and some kill them just for fun.
Did we ever know that they are our allies
who are trying to help us as they can?
They aerate the soil for plants to grow,
thus helping the plants to absorb nutrients.
If those troops of ants were not here on earth,
the recycling of soil nutrients would not happen,
and plants would not produce the food
animals and humans need,
making all of us starve to death.
How ruthless and stupid are we to kill ants
which are working to help us survive!
How beautiful and lovable are the ants!

Look at the much-hated termites!
They are notorious for eating up the rafters,
doors, and windows of our houses.
They are the decomposers of wood and litter.
In the process, they make the soil fertile.
They are nature's recyclers.
They are working hard for our survival.
How helpful are the termites!

Look at the honeybees!
They give us sweet honey
and pollinate most fruits and vegetables.
Without them there would be no fruits and vegetables.
Our agricultural fields, vegetable gardens,
and plates would be empty without them.
They work hard as they are programmed to do.
How beneficial to us are the honeybees!

Look at the nocturnal bats!
We label them as harbingers of infectious diseases
and as such we view them as unwelcome guests in our yards.

But we are ignorant of heaven's deputation for these bats,
as they are the pollinators of plants and flowers that bloom at night.
These plants would be extinct
if the bats were not there to pollinate them.
We would not be able to eat mangoes,
bananas, cocoa and guava,
as all of them are plants which are pollinated at night by bats.
There would be no chocolate or chocolate drinks
if these bats were not there,
for they are the nocturnal pollinators
of all these much-wanted fruity plants.
They are also insectivorous,
mainly eating the much-hated mosquito.
Are we not stupid to hate the bats
who do such a wonderful job to help us?

Finally, what about the much-hated rats?
They are aerators of soil
and spread seeds in the forests and plantations.
Due to their abundance
and physiological and genetic similarities with humans
they are the fulcrum for biomedical researchers
using them to find all kinds of vaccines
and medicines for us humans.
They are the scapegoats for our vaccines.
We really owe them a lot.
Are we hard-hearted not to thank them
for the self-immolating job they do for us?

Who assigned these meaningful duties
to all these seemingly worthless animals, from ant to elephant?
Who mechanized them to do these jobs
with such meticulous and unfailing precision?
Who is behind the rationale of these irrational creatures,
each contributing in their own valuable role?
Who is behind the rationality of the rational actions

of the irrational beings working for purposeful ends,
and for the common good of the welfare of mankind?
Is it chance or design? Or are we blind within ourselves?

Let us be kind to the birds and the ants,
the worms, the wasps, the bees, and the fish,
and the monkeys and the nocturnal bats,
and thousands of such animals on earth.
Let us learn to love and respect them for their selfless work.

Gratitude is the mother of virtues.
If there is no mother, there are no children.
Ingratitude is a vice, as gratitude is a virtue.
Ingratitude toward God or man in any form is a vice.
Ingratitude toward God is called irreligion.
Ingratitude entails dereliction of duty.
Ingratitude entails unpaid debt.
Ingratitude entails covert injustice.
Ingratitude entails obliquity.
Ingratitude entails narcissism,
which eventually hurls one into dire desolation.
Let me not be ungrateful!

What can I return to you, my Lord and my God,
for creating different types of beings on earth,
each with its own purposeful role to perform,
to aid the humans to live a cozy life on earth?

Turn away your eyes from my sins:
of breaking thy very first and third commandments
by not acknowledging your mercy
of creating these little animals to help me
and for maintaining them for endless years,
and also for breaking the seventh by not
appreciating what they do for me.

Grant me the grace to see your hands
when I see birds flying in V squadrons in the sky.
Grant me the grace to appreciate your thoughtful design
in creating rats, rabbits, and guinea pigs
when I receive my vaccinations.
Grant me the grace to see your ingenious design
behind the creation of ants and worms and bees.
Grant me the grace not to tramp and kill an ant
just for fun or amusement when I see them on the ground.
Grant me the grace to think that I am an ant for you
if I ever think of tramping an ant for fun.
Grant me the grace to wonder at your care,
seeing how you have created thousands of
birds and animals and other animate beings
to make earth habitable for all humans.
Grant me the grace to see your purposeful design
in every creature that inhabits the earth.

What thanks can I offer you, my Lord and my God,
for all the birds and animals,
from the little sparrows to the big elephants,
that you have thoughtfully designed
to make life inhabitable for humans on earth
as a boon out of your love and mercy?
I will laud your name, my Lord and my God,
I will chant and applaud your name forever.

23

Trees: The Silent Benefactors

Wherever you turn your head,
whether it is to the left or right,
to the front or back,
up to the mountaintops or down to the valleys or creeks,
you see trees, bushes, and shrubs,
in various sizes, heights, shapes, and colors.
They are in gardens, lawns, parks, and forests,
as they are ubiquitous on earth.
Have you ever wondered what they do up here?

Part II

They help to remove the carbon dioxide
which all animals release into the atmosphere.
They control climate by removing the excess
carbon dioxide from the atmosphere.
They produce oxygen through photosynthesis
thus providing us the vital gas needed for our existence.
They filter the dust particles in the air.
They improve the quality of air around us.
They help with soil erosion
and mark the changing of the seasons.
They preserve soil and conserve the forests.
They remove and store carbon.
They provide the habitat for wildlife.
They provide the habitat for insects
and many parasites and parasitic plants.

Their leaves serve as food for animals.
They provide us with food in the form of fruits and grains.
They provide fuel for cooking and heating.
They provide shade and shelter.
They are the poor man's umbrella during rainstorms.
Trees support the hammocks of the pompous
and the wooden swings of the poor.
They provide materials
for the construction of furniture and buildings.

Imagine an earth without trees and plants:
We would have no oxygen to breathe.
There would be no food for animals.
There would be no food for humans.
We can forget about life existing on earth,
as everything would have been different
since nothing can survive without trees and plants.

Gratitude is the mother of virtues.
If there is no mother, there are no children.

Ingratitude is a vice, as gratitude is a virtue.
Ingratitude toward God or man in any form is a vice.
Ingratitude toward God is called irreligion.
Ingratitude entails dereliction of duty.
Ingratitude entails unpaid debt.
Ingratitude entails covert injustice.
Ingratitude entails obliquity.
Ingratitude entails narcissism,
which eventually hurls one into dire desolation.
Let me not be ungrateful!

What can I return to you, my Lord and my God,
for creating the shrubs, bushes, and trees,
the scaffolding for our life on earth,
and for sustaining them as long as the earth?

Turn away your eyes from my sins:
of breaking thy very first and third commandments
by not acknowledging your purpose
for creating the trees, shrubs, and plants,
and also for breaking the seventh by not
preserving and taking care of them.

Grant me the grace to thank the trees
when I sit on chairs and sofas and eat my meals at tables.
Grant me the grace to think of thy care
when I avoid the sun and rain in the shade of trees,
the natural umbrellas of the poor.
Grant me the grace to thank the trees
when I sit cozily in my house,
which is largely made of wood,
protecting me from rain and the sun's heat.
Grant me the grace to thank you for your wisdom
when I breathe in oxygen.
Grant me the grace to plant a tree
so that the next generation can breathe well too.

Part II

Grant me the grace to think of your bounty,
of creating different types of fruit trees and plants,
when I eat fruits and grains of trees and plants.

What thanks can I offer you, my Lord and my God,
for the precious trees and bushes,
and for sustaining their growth over the centuries
as a boon out of your mercy and care?
I will laud your name, my Lord and my God,
I will chant and applaud your name forever.

24

The Mountains: The Top of the World

When driving your car through the countryside,
or while sitting in the window seat of a plane,
or while travelling across the country by train,
have you ever gazed upon the mountain ranges,
and the hillocks and valleys and dales silhouetted
against the horizons with clouds in their lap?

Have you ever wondered why these useless
mountains are there, filling the horizon?
If you are a nature-lover you might at least enjoy
the beauty and abundance of nature.
If not, the chain of mountains for you
might just be a heap or mount of useless terrain.

If you think so, you are terribly mistaken.
The Designer of the universe has given
them important and specific jobs to do.
They are the habitats for animals and plants.
They are the water fountains of the world.
They are the cradles of rivers and forests.
They hold water, ice, and snow.
They are the source for potable water supplies.
They host a quarter of earth's forests.
They host many diverse animals and birds.
They are the home of many tribal and indigenous peoples.
They are the grazing land for animals.
They are the cradle of many food crops.

The mountain ranges are the natural paradise of the world,
revealing the unparalleled beauty of nature.
They stop and divert winds and clouds,
making air cool enough to induce rain.
They stop the passage of clouds,
making rain fall on the windward side,
sending water gushing through steep streams and rivulets
providing water for domestic, industrial, and irrigation purposes.
Damming of valley rivers between mountains
stores water for hydroelectric projects,
for flash flood controls, and for water storage.

If there were no mountains and valleys:
There would be no dams.
There would be no water reservoirs.
There would be no conservation of water.
There would be no hydroelectric projects.
There would be less electricity.
There would be no planned irrigation.
There would be less crop production.
There would be less water for domestic usage.
There would be fewer forests.

There would be no flood control.
Life on earth would be much different.

Gratitude is the mother of virtues.
If there is no mother, there are no children.
Ingratitude is a vice, as gratitude is a virtue.
Ingratitude toward God or man in any form is a vice.
Ingratitude toward God is called irreligion.
Ingratitude entails dereliction of duty.
Ingratitude entails unpaid debt.
Ingratitude entails covert injustice.
Ingratitude entails obliquity.
Ingratitude entails narcissism,
which eventually hurls one into dire desolation.
Let me not be ungrateful!

What can I return to you, my Lord and my God,
for creating the mountains, hillocks, hummocks,
hills, valleys, dales, vales, rivulets, streams, and rivers,
each with its own role to play to make earth inhabitable?

Turn away your eyes from my sins:
of breaking thy very first and third commandments
by not acknowledging your purpose
of creating the mountains and hills and dales,
and also for breaking the seventh by not
preserving and taking care of them.

Grant me the grace to see your hands
behind the mist-veiled mountain ranges.
Grant me the grace to see your wisdom
in creating the hills and dales.
Grant me the grace to see your beauty,
sleeping in the laps of mountains
and reflecting in creeks and streams

that gorge down from the crest to the bottom,
carrying much-needed goodies for the valley dwellers.

What thanks can I offer you, my Lord and my God,
for the precious mountains and hillocks,
and the brooks and streams that flow from them,
as a boon out of your mercy and care?
I will laud your name, my Lord and my God,
I will chant and applaud your name forever.

Part III

*"But if you turn your face away, they will be disturbed.
You will take away their breath, and they will fail,
and they will return to their dust. You will send
forth your Spirit, and they will be created. And you will
renew the face of the earth."*[1]

1. Ps 103:29–30 (CPDV).

25

Creation and Sustenance: Ex Nihilo Nihil Fit

Long, long ago, before the dawn of time,
there was a tiny speck,
with no length or width or height,
or with any type of seen or unseen dimensions.

It was an invisible speck of unknown location,
a speck which no one knew whence it came or how it appeared,
a speck of unknown composition and origin.

Part III

One day this enigmatic, mysterious speck
exploded and inflated with unimaginable force.
It resulted in an ever-expanding universe of
ever-accelerating expansion,
and in the dark matter which makes up most matter in the universe,
which we call the elusive and very mysterious black hole,
which contains the elusive dark energy.

The Big Bang caused an ever-expanding, interstellar void,
and it resulted in ever-expanding nebulae of superclusters,
with unimaginable spans of millions of light years.
These superclusters contain millions of clusters
of galaxies which are of different size and shape,
with dwarf galaxies with millions of stars
and with giant galaxies with trillions of stars.
Each of the galaxies contains millions of stars,
with many stars shining in the sky,
with a retinue of planets and the planets' retinue of moons.

All these started with the teeny, tiny speck;
or was it something else that inflated?
The truth is that no one knows what happened,
and even the Big Bang is mere speculation.
The truth is the origin of the universe is not within man's grasp.
It lies within the domain of the Almighty.

The only obvious thing we know from science and observation
is that there are stars and galaxies and clusters of galaxies,
and superclusters of galaxies with trillions of stars,
with trillions of light years of void space
between the galaxies and clusters and superclusters,
and all are flying away from each other.
There is the speculation of the Big Bang,
but the origin of all this is hidden from us.

We know that we are real,
and the sun and the moon and the stars are real,
and the galaxies and void spaces are real,
but we do not know how this happened.
So, let us go with the Big Bang
and speculate that all happened from the inflation of a speck:
Ex nihilo nihil fit, i.e. nothing comes out of nothingness.

From where did the little speck come?
It could not have generated itself, for we know
nothing can cause itself into existence by itself.
It could not be there by chance,
for it was a mindless speck,
a speck of matter without reason.
It could not be there by necessity,
for it was a contingent speck whose existence was not needed.
This could not have originated from another speck;
if so, from where did that another speck come?

So, this speck was made out of nothingness,
by an omnipotent power whom we call God,
who loaded this speck with massive potentiality
and transformed that potentiality into actuality,
to form all other visible things in the world,
with all entities and beings programmed
to evolve in time as he programmed it
for as long as his providence sustains it,
just as we put the ignition key in its slot
and give it a turn to start the car,
and after going through hundreds of sequential
and intricate electrical, mechanical, hydraulic,
pneumatic, telematic circuits and systems actuations,
the car runs on the road, passing miles and miles and miles,
for as long as the driver sits on the seat.
The human mind designed the car.
The omniscient Almighty designed the universe.

Gratitude is the mother of virtues.
If there is no mother, there are no children.
Ingratitude is a vice, as gratitude is a virtue.
Ingratitude toward God or man in any form is a vice.
Ingratitude toward God is called irreligion.
Ingratitude entails dereliction of duty.
Ingratitude entails unpaid debt.
Ingratitude entails covert injustice.
Ingratitude entails obliquity.
Ingratitude entails narcissism,
which eventually hurls one into dire desolation.
Let me not be ungrateful!

What can I return to you, my Lord and my God,
for creating this ever-expanding universe,
and for sustaining its existence
with your merciful providence?

Turn away your eyes from my sins
of breaking thy very first and third commandments
by not acknowledging the creation of
this wonderful universe and sustaining it
with your infinite mercy despite dire ingratitude.

Grant me the grace to see your hands
behind the stars that are scattered all around the sky.
Grant me the grace to gaze into the cerulean sky
and see your spirit behind the stars in the nocturnal sky.
Grant me the grace to think of your wisdom
when I see white, yellow, blue, and red stars.
Grant me the grace to remember that the starry sky I see everyday
is not the same now as it was millennia ago.
Grant me the grace to wonder at the vastness of the universe,
and to muse on you who scattered the billions of stars all around,
suspended in the nothingness of vast space,
and mechanized their expansion in such a way

that none of them collide with one another,
which would wreak havoc throughout the universe.
Grant me the grace to believe in you and your ways
which are beyond the grasp of my reason.
Grant me the grace to grasp through faith
what my human senses fail to understand
about the creation of the universe
and the evolution of everything in it.

What thanks can I offer you, my Lord and my God,
for the ingenious design of the vast universe,
with millions of galaxies and trillions of stars,
each following its own evolution and path,
and for sustaining their existence,
sticking to your purposeful mechanization?
I will laud your name, my Lord and my God,
I will chant and applaud your name forever.

26

Motion and Sustenance: The Unmoved Mover

A flying bullet has a shooter behind it.
A moving car has an engine and driver behind it.
A flying plane has a pilot and flight crew behind it.
A flung stone has a thrower behind it.
A moving cloud has wind behind it.
A blowing wind has a pressure difference behind it.
An erupting volcano has a pressure underneath.
Anything in motion has something behind it.
There is nothing in the world subject to senses,
that moves without a cause or propelling force.

Who is behind the growth of a tree?
Who is behind the movement of my hands?
Who is behind when I make a decision?
Who is behind when I choose to do something?
When the heart stops, I cannot move:
If I were moving the heart, I would restart it.
But since I cannot do that
it means I am not the one moving my heart.
So the cause of my existence is someone else,
and I can exist and move only so long as
he exerts his influence on me to move.

Who is behind the rotation of earth?
Who is behind the revolution of earth?
Who is behind the motion of revolving planets?
Who is behind the motion of revolving moons?
Who is behind the motion of galaxies?
Who is behind the motion of galaxy clusters?
Who is behind the motion of superclusters?

Since the cause of their movement is not in them
they will stop moving
when the one who sustains their movement
stops sustaining their motion.
So, everything that moves will stop
when the mover stops acting on them,
just as a car stops when the driver
stops giving gasoline to the engine.

If we answer that the Big Bang is behind the motions of
moons, planets, stars, galaxies and superclusters of galaxies,
then the question is: Who caused the Big Bang to bang so big
to set that ever-expanding universe in motion,
with each moon and planet and stars and galaxies
following meticulous and unfailing paths?

Part III

Can such meticulous motions,
with such purposeful goals,
result by chance from a chaotic bang?
Can the motions of superclusters, galaxies, and stars,
and the rotation and revolution of planets such as the earth,
in specified unfailing orbits for millennia,
without a hitch, collision, or wreck of any kind,
result from an unplanned, chaotic bang,
when meticulously planned and executed strikes
by veteran and expert billiard players
often cause unplanned, unintended, and random
strikes, shunts, and collisions of many billiard balls?

The unmoved Prime Mover initiated the Big Bang,
for we know that nothing moves without a mover,
and the purposeful order in the universe shows
the immaculate design of the Prime Mover.
He exerts his ongoing influence
for the sustenance of all that he created,
and without such sustenance
everything would vanish into nothingness.

Gratitude is the mother of virtues.
If there is no mother, there are no children.
Ingratitude is a vice, as gratitude is a virtue.
Ingratitude toward God or man in any form is a vice.
Ingratitude toward God is called irreligion.
Ingratitude entails dereliction of duty.
Ingratitude entails unpaid debt.
Ingratitude entails covert injustice.
Ingratitude entails obliquity.
Ingratitude entails narcissism,
which eventually hurls one into dire desolation.
Let me not be ungrateful!

What can I return you, my Lord and my God,
for setting everything in ordered motion,
the motions of all the seen and unseen celestial bodies,
and for sustaining that motion at your will.

Turn away your eyes from my sins
of breaking thy very first and third commandments
by not acknowledging the initiation of all the motions
in the universe and mechanizing to sustain it
with your infinite mercy despite dire ingratitude.

Grant me the grace to thank you
for setting the world in motion.
Grant me the grace to see your hands
behind the motion of every celestial body.
Grant me the grace to grasp the unfolding of events
which are beyond the realm of science.
Grant me the grace to thank you
for sustaining the universe every second.
Grant me the grace to thank you
for setting my life in motion.
Grant me the grace to thank you
for sustaining my life every second.
Grant me the grace to grasp through faith
what my human senses fail to understand about
the orderly motions of all celestial bodies and
thy wonderful initiation of motion in the universe.

What thanks can I offer you, my Lord and my God,
for setting the world in motion,
and for setting everything in it in motion,
and for keeping everything in motion
because if you were to forget about sustaining the motion
of even the littlest sparrows for one second
they would vanish into nothingness?
I will laud your name, my Lord and my God,
I will chant and applaud your name forever.

Part IV

*"Be merciful to me, O God, according to your great mercy.
And, according to the plentitude of your compassion,
wipe out my iniquity. Wash me once again from my iniquity,
and cleanse me from my sin. For I know my iniquity,
and my sin is ever before me. Against you only have I sinned,
and I have done evil before your eyes. And so, you are
justified in your words, and you will prevail when you
give judgment. For behold, I was conceived in iniquities,
and in sinfulness did my mother conceive me.
For behold, you have loved truth. The obscure and hidden
things of your wisdom, you have manifested to me.
You will sprinkle me with hyssop, and I will be cleansed.
You will wash me, and I will be made whiter than snow.
In my hearing, you will grant gladness and rejoicing.
And the bones that have been humbled will exult.
Turn your face away from my sins, and erase all my iniquities.
Create a clean heart in me, O God. And renew an
upright spirit within my inmost being. Do not cast
me away from your face; and do not take your Holy Spirit
from me. Restore to me the joy of your salvation,
and confirm me with an unsurpassed spirit."*[1]

1. Ps 50:3–14 (CPDV).

27

The Cross of Christ: Attunement of Human Will

If I were Christ the Redeemer,
when they came to arrest me in Gethsemane,
I would have invoked a flight of Virtues.
And, lifting my arms up,
would have lifted the retinue of soldiers fifty feet in the air,
for people to see them,
and all would see and believe that I am the mighty God.

If I were Christ the Redeemer,
when they shouted, *Crucify Him,*
I would have made them stand still as statues,
with clenched fist and open mouth,
forever and ever
so that the world would see
and believe that I am the omnipotent God indeed.

If I were Christ the Redeemer,
when Pilate was going to say *Ecce Homo,*
I would have invoked a host of Powers
and would have made him deaf and mute,
that he would not be able to judge me.
I would also have made him a quadriplegic
so that he would not sign the verdict either,
and the whole world would have
stood in awe and shouted that I am God indeed.

Part IV

If I were Christ the Redeemer,
when they put the crown of thorns on me,
I would have transformed that thorny crown
into a golden tiara, studded with costly diamonds,
so that they would have been petrified at my power.

If I were Christ the Redeemer,
when they gave me the cross to carry,
I would have converted it into a golden throne,
canopied and embedded with gleaming diamonds,
that they would tremble with awe at my power.

If I were Christ the Redeemer,
when they made me carry my cross to Calvary
I would have invoked a host of Thrones[1] from above,
who would have flown my throne in the air
so that the world would stand in disbelief,
believing in me and in the God who sent me.

If I were Christ the Redeemer,
when they nailed me to the cross
I would have made the earth they stood on
yield and disappear into the nether world,
and I would have made a million angels
descend from the heavens,
blowing trumpets and beating drums,
and I would have ascended into the heavens
amidst them in all glory, splendor, pomp, and blare.
And seeing such an unbelievable sight,
all the people would have fallen to the ground,
panicked and fear-stricken at my power,
and adoring me, the Almighty God!

---

1. According to Christian angelology, Thrones are the third highest order of angels. They are the creatures that function as chariots of God driven by Cherubs.

What do you think Jesus prayed in Gethsemane
that he even had hematohidrosis
on account of extreme mental anguish?

He was praying not to fall into various kinds of temptation.
He was praying not to fall into the temptation
of allowing his weak human flesh
to overcome his human will's acceptance of the cross.
He was praying not to fall into the temptation
of invoking his divine powers to overcome
the horrible persecution he was going to undergo.
He was praying to God the Father to give him the strength
to bear the crucifixion as a human being.
He was praying for the strength for his human will
to attune to God's will, which the flesh wanted to evade.

The agony of Jesus is not him dying on the cross:
It is not Jesus being condemned by Pilate.
It is not Jesus bearing the flagellations.
It is not Jesus wearing the thorny crown.
It is not Jesus carrying the cross.
It is not Jesus meeting mother Mary.
It is not Jesus falling due to hypovolemic shock.
It is not Jesus being nailed to the cross.
It is not Jesus dying of thirst.
It is not Jesus crying out of ostensible despair.
It is not Jesus crying out of ostensible desolation.
It is not Jesus dying on the cross.

The agony is the silence of Jesus.
It is the passive inaction of Jesus.
It is the passive submissiveness of Jesus.
It is the ostensible incompetence of Jesus.
It is Jesus' silence when questioned by Pilate.
It is taking the judgement of Pilate,
even though he could have turned it around.

It is Jesus' acceptance of the cross,
which he could have easily averted.
It is warding off the temptation to invoke
his divine powers during the afflictions of via crucis.
It is overpowering the mental anguish,
which is much more than the physical anguish.
It is accepting the thorny crown,
even though he could have averted it.
It is carrying the cross,
even though he could have averted it.
It is falling under the weight of the cross,
even though he could have averted it.
It is being nailed to the cross,
even though he could have averted it.
It is dying on the cross,
even though he could have averted it.
These are the last miracles Jesus performed
before his death because he needed
superhuman power to do these things
without invoking and obtaining
divine powers from heaven above.

This is where the fallen Cherubim's
plans fell asunder for a second time,
when Jesus embraced the cross
without invoking his divine powers.

When somebody kicks us,
it is quite easy to kick back and be the winner,
but it takes superhuman power not to react.
When somebody slaps us on the face,
it is quite easy to slap back harder and be the winner,
but it takes superhuman power not to react.
When somebody spits at us,
it is quite easy spit back and be the winner,
but it takes superhuman power not to react.

When somebody scorns us
it is quite easy to retaliate and be the winner,
but it takes superhuman power not to react.
When somebody stabs us in the back,
it is quite easy to stab back and be the winner,
but it takes superhuman power not to react.
When somebody cheats us,
it is quite easy to retaliate and be the winner,
but it takes superhuman power not to react.
When somebody yells at us,
it is quite easy to yell back louder and be the winner,
but it takes superhuman power not to react.
When somebody screams at us
it is quite easy to scream back louder and be the winner,
but it takes superhuman power not to react.
When somebody hurts our feelings with words,
it is quite easy to hurt their feelings as well,
but it takes superhuman power
to take it in, bleed in the heart, and show
an unperturbed countenance outside,
just as a captain stays calm and quiet in the battlefield
amid flying bullets, roaring planes, and exploding shells.

Why did Jesus embrace the cross,
which he could have easily avoided?
The cross was not thrust upon him.
He anticipated and was looking forward to it.
He wanted to sacrifice himself for our salvation,
and there is no better love one can show for another
than by laying down one's own life for others.
It is because he wanted to redeem our souls.
He wanted to show us the way to heaven.
He wanted to show us how to carry the cross,
which he told us to take up and follow him.
He was showing us that the way to heaven
is the way of crosses and not of roses.

Part IV

Jesus did not carry the cross to go to heaven,
because he was already from heaven.
Jesus did not carry the cross to evade hell
because he is the master who created hell and heaven.
Jesus carried the cross because he really loved us.
Even if a mother does not know how to swim,
if her child falls into a lake, she would jump to save the child,
without even thinking of her own life,
not to go to heaven or to evade the hell,
but because she loves her child more than herself.

Gratitude is the mother of virtues.
If there is no mother, there are no children.
Ingratitude is a vice, as gratitude is a virtue.
Ingratitude toward God or man in any form is a vice.
Ingratitude toward God is called irreligion.
Ingratitude entails dereliction of duty.
Ingratitude entails unpaid debt.
Ingratitude entails covert injustice.
Ingratitude entails obliquity.
Ingratitude entails narcissism,
which eventually hurls one into dire desolation.
Let me not be ungrateful!

What can I return to you, my Lord and my God,
for redeeming me and showing me
how to carry my crosses in this life and
how to follow you to your kingdom carrying my cross?

Turn away your eyes from our sins of not seeking
and attuning our human will to your will
and thus breaking all your ten commandments,
making us unworthy to enter your kingdom.

Breaking the first commandment through displaying:
irreligion, disbelief, despair, selfishness, apostasy,

presumption, indifference, sloth, idolatry, sacrilege,
simony, agnosticism, atheism, ingratitude,
superstitions, sorcery, spiritism, and more.

Breaking the second commandment through displaying:
false oaths, perjury, blasphemy,
not keeping vows made in Christian sacraments,
and adopting unchristian names to hide Christian
identity in order to evade evangelization.

Breaking the third commandment by:
not keeping Sundays and holy days of obligation,
depriving our souls of their spiritual food,
and making such days full workdays to make money,
or to entertain the senses with fun and jubilation.

Breaking the fourth commandment by:
not obeying parents, teachers, and clergy,
not supporting parents and neighbors in need,
not being grateful to our parents,
evading the duty of procreation,
not bringing up children as they should be,
not showing filial piety.

Breaking the fifth commandment through:
homicide, infanticide, abortion, suicide, scandal,
euthanasia, terrorism, intemperance, drugs,
violence, shootings, medical overdoses,
gluttony, stealing time, killing time.

Breaking the sixth commandment through:
conjugal infidelity, separation, divorce, incest,
free union, trial marriage, masturbation, seduction,
adultery, prostitution, rape, same-sex marriage,
pornography, lust, intemperance.

Part IV

Breaking the seventh commandment by engaging in:
communism, capitalism, socialism, systemic
inequality, theft, corruption, waste, slavery,
approving unjust wages, exploitation,
intemperance, eavesdropping,
usurping power, fraud, gambling, discrimination,
disregarding the poor, being apathetic toward nature,
inordinate and excessive affection toward pets.

Breaking the eighth commandment by:
making rash judgments, calumny, slander, flattery,
lying, false witnessing, perjury,
divulging professional and personal secrets,
adopting clandestine Christian names.

Breaking the ninth commandment through:
the lust of eyes, the lust of flesh, thinking impure thoughts,
tarnished vision, having an unchaste tongue, seduction.

Breaking the tenth commandment by displaying or engaging in:
greed, avarice, envy, jealousy, lust,
robbery, theft, fraud, misusing and usurping talents,
attachment to worldly goods/positions/fame.

> During the oppeese, the prayer for the dead,
> the St. Thomas Christians sing:
>
> *"Karthave nin kurisine jnan*
> *Aaraathichu vanangunnu*
> *Athuthan jnangalkuthanam*
> *Rakshayum uyirum nalkunnu."*[2]
> *(O Lord, we adore and venerate your cross,*
> *because it is our resurrection*
> *and it gives us life and salvation.)*

---

2. Syromalabar Church, *Syromalabar Sabhayude Qurbana Kramam*, 205.

Our Lord Jesus Christ again reminds us
about the importance of carrying one's own cross.

> *"If anyone is willing to come after me,*
> *let him deny himself, and take up his cross,*
> *and follow me."*[3]

So what is the cross Jesus was talking about?
What cross does Jesus want me to take up in order to follow him?
Where can I find the cross to carry and follow Jesus?
What is the cross I must adore and venerate?
If I can find that cross, I will surely carry it!

Is it the Latin cross or the Greek cross?
Is it the Jerusalem cross or the Byzantine cross?
Is it the anchor cross or the Calvary cross?
Is it the Celtic cross or the Maltese cross?
Is it the St. Thomas cross or the Marian cross?
Is it the East Syrian cross or the West Syrian cross?
Is it the Armenian cross or the Coptic cross?
Is it the St John cross or the Canterbury cross?

Is it the wooden cross of Calvary on which Jesus died?
Or is it some other wooden cross?
Or is it any cross which is the symbol of Christianity?
Or is it the golden cross carried in the front of funeral
processions of the rich, the famous, and the pompous?
Or is it the silver cross carried in the front of funeral
processions of the middle class or the common man?
Or is it the wooden cross carried in the front of funeral
processions of the poor and the destitute,
who have no money for the golden or silver crosses?
Or is it the cross that I see atop church steeples?
Or is it the cross that I see atop church spires?
Or is it the cross that I see over the tabernacle?
Or is it the cross that I see over the monstrance?

3. Matt 16:24 (CPDV).

Part IV

All of these crosses are just symbols
of the real cross that was given to me by God.

The following are the crosses I must adore, venerate, and carry,
without mumbling, just like Jesus did.
Even if I can avert it, I should carry it like him:
so that I can be the image and likeness of God,
so that by suffering for others I prove my love for neighbor,
so that I follow Christ, carrying my cross to the end,
so that I do not have to face St. Peter at heaven's gate,
without a cross to barter for the entry into heaven.

Grant me the grace not to dodge my cross
of the ruthless and unhelpful spouse.
Grant me the grace not to dodge my crosses
of demanding and narcissistic children.
Grant me the grace not to dodge my crosses
of stubborn and obstinate parents.
Grant me the grace not to dodge my crosses
of senile, infirm, and feeble parents.
Grant me the grace not to dodge my crosses
of forfeiting a part of my life for my children.
Grant me the grace not to dodge my crosses
of forfeiting a part of my life for my parents.
Grant me the grace not to dodge my crosses
of children born with congenital deformities.
Grant me the grace not to dodge my crosses
of bearing and rearing children for God.
Grant me the grace not to dodge my crosses
of putting up with my step-parents.
Grant me the grace not to dodge my crosses
of putting up with my mean half-siblings.
Grant me the grace not to dodge my crosses
of putting up with my jealous in-laws.
Grant me the grace not to dodge my crosses
of dealing with my envious neighbors.

Grant me the grace not to dodge my crosses
of education by quitting college
or by switching to easier subjects.
Grant me the grace not to dodge my cross
of working to make my livelihood
by living on public welfare all my life.
Grant me the grace not to dodge my cross
of working to make my livelihood
by doing something stupid to get into prisons,
the resorts lacking only swimming pools,
so that I can live without working all my life.
Grant me the grace not to dodge my crosses
of helping family, friends, and strangers.
Grant me the strength not to dodge my crosses
of poverty, tribulations, and afflictions.
Grant me the grace not to dodge my crosses
of my own weaknesses and shortcomings.
Grant me the grace not to dodge my crosses
of forgiving those who offend me
as it is in forgiving that I am forgiven.
Grant me the grace not to dodge my cross
of bearing a true Christian name,
thus evangelizing Christianity through my name.
Grant me the grace not to dodge the cross of evangelization
by giving sugar-coated and clandestine
Christian names to my children
to hide their Christian identity,
which is tantamount to apostasy.
Grant me the grace not to name my children in
such way that people have to look up the dictionary
to find out their religious affiliation,
which is tantamount to apostasy.

Grant me the grace to stay unperturbed and silent
amidst the treacherous trials and vicissitudes of life.
Grant me the grace not to reach in front of St. Peter

with emptied hands after forsaking all crosses.
Grant me the grace not to think that because God is merciful
I can attain heaven without any merit.
Grant me the grace to accept crosses of
my own shortcomings and concupiscence.
Grant me the grace to put a helping finger
on another's cross before he falls.
Grant me the grace not to refuse a free COVID-19 vaccine
because of my selfishness and intention to wait and see
what side effects befall those who have already taken it.
Grant me the grace to help my nearest and dearest
as I can while they are around me and alive,
and not to run around buying costly wreaths and flowers
and offering solemn requiem masses at death anniversaries,
years after they are dead and gone forever.
Grant me the grace not to assume that I can go to heaven
by praying, adoring, venerating, and flattering God,
without putting into practice what I pray.
Grant me the grace to understand that prayer is no more
the soul of religion if it has caved to lip service.
Grant me the grace to discern that prayer without heart
is a self-defense mechanism of the egotistic mind.
Grant me the grace to understand that prayers
which are not put into practice in real life
are the opium of the soul which falsely assure heaven
and yet in reality are psychedelics given by Satan.

Grant me the grace not to show bell, book, and candle
to those who raise constructive criticism.
Grant me the grace to spend my time wisely
to manage my flock's spiritual needs
rather than church's material needs.
Grant me the grace not to follow Johan Tetzel
hiding behind the shade of the sacrosanct cross.
Grant me the grace to be that shepherd
that goes around the parochial pastures,

looking for the fallen and maimed sheep,
to nurse and take them back to the sheepfold.
Grant me the grace not to be a master, but a servant.
Grant me the grace not to be that shepherd
that ignores or refuses services for impecunious sheep.

Grant me the grace to discern that the riches and wealth
which are showered on me will turn into Satan's baits
unless I pass them on to others as they come to me.
Grant me the grace to remember that whatever I do
to those around me are done to you above.
Grant me the grace to understand that
I am not praying for God, but for myself.
Grant me the grace to hug my real-life crosses
before I venerate and adore the symbolic crosses.
Grant me the grace not to leave my real crosses at home,
such as sick parents or a spouse with a broken leg,
and run to churches to adore and venerate
the glittering golden and the shiny silver crosses there.
Grant me the grace not to substitute my real crosses
with the inanimate symbolic crosses at churches.
Grant me the grace not to be hypocritical and sacrilegious
by adoring and kissing the crosses at churches
after inclemently kicking out my real-life crosses.
Grant me the strength to discern and do your will.

Grant me the grace to meditate on the meaning of the cross
and to find out the real crosses which I must carry.
Grant me the grace to remember and find
the crosses I have evaded or dropped,
and the strength to return,
pick them up,
and carry them just as Jesus did.
Grant me the grace to follow the shepherd
through the imitation of Christ by carrying
my crosses without evading and grudging.

Part IV

Grant me the grace not to waste my time searching for you
above the cerulean sky, or behind the silvery clouds,
or beneath the horizon, or behind the moon or twinkling stars,
or above the cathedral ceilings of the holy churches,
or inside the golden tabernacle, or in the gilded monstrance,
when you are found in the needy who surround me.
Grant me the grace not to kneel and stare at you
as you sit afar on the altar inside the golden monstrance,
when you are within me through the Holy Communion,
and this is tantamount to a host who ignores the invited guest
inside the house by standing outside the house
waiting for the arrival of the same guest.
Grant me the grace not to praise you with orans hands or
clapping hands if I am too blinded by self-absorption
to see your image and likeness in my relatives,
and the needy who are right here under my nose.

Grant me the grace to understand that
through my ceaseless and vain lip service
I cannot be in communion with
God the Father or God the Son,
or with God the Holy Spirit,
or with Our Lady or St. Joseph,
or with Seraphim, Cherubim, or other angelic orders,
or with the known and unknown spirits in the heavens,
unless I am in communion with my relatives,
friends, neighbors, and other human beings,
and all other animate and inanimate beings on earth.
Grant me the grace not to be a hypocritical prayerholic,
trying to endear the unseen and unknown powers
while estranging the seen, dear, and near around me
to selfishly attain to that blessed abode of heaven
by trying to hoodwink God himself and all his retinue
through effortless lip service, which costs me nothing.

Prayers are like hypocritical fig trees with lot of leaves,
but no fruits beneath the branches to satiate the hungry.
Unless churches, temples, gurdwaras, mosques,
synagogues, and other religious places of worship
make man a better human being within himself,
and discourage all forms of religious fanaticism,
they are to be deemed as the fallen Cherubim's
Trojan horses inside the City of God.
As peoples get smarter, wiser, and richer,
they bog deeper and deeper into selfishness and social evils,
running away from the very goal of salvation.

Grant me the grace to spread the Gospel of God
to those who have not yet heard about it,
as Christianity stands unique from other religions.
Some religions do not have founders.
Some religions do not have a god.
Some religions foster religious intolerance,
and some religions foster terrorism,
all of which are tantamount to undermining
the purpose of religion itself.
Christianity is a universal religion
as churches are open to all for worship
irrespective of race, religion, creed, or caste.
None of the religious founders ever claimed,
save Jesus Christ, that any of them was God himself:
Jesus said to him: "I am the Way, and the
Truth, and the Life. No one comes to the Father, except
through me."[4]
All other religious founders gave precepts to follow, but
none said *Follow me* as Jesus said.

Grant me the grace not to mar your image and likeness
within me by not carrying my own crosses.
Grant me the grace to see your image and likeness

4. John 14:6 (CPDV).

in others around me and to be a Simon of Cyrene for them.
Grant me the grace to understand that
I can only follow to where you went
by carrying my own crosses to the Calvary of my death,
and not by just pitying you through your *via crucis*
by partaking and singing in the stations of the cross.

Grant me the grace to grasp that
the cross is the symbol of sacrifice,
and sacrifice is the symbol of love,
and love is God or God is love,
and while carrying my cross
I am manifesting your image and likeness on earth
and accepting your image and likeness
in the persons for whom I am carrying the cross.
Grant me the grace to carry the crosses of my life
and follow in your footsteps.

During the tenth station of the cross,
the St. Thomas Christians sing:

> *"Vyrikal thingi varunnente chuttilum*
> *Khoramaam garjanangal*
> *Bhaagicheduthente vasthrangal ellam*
> *Paapikal vyrikal"*[5]
> *(The enemies thronged around me screaming,*
> *and the vile sinners divided my clothes among themselves.)*

No army can have two generals.
No ship can have two captains.
No car can have two drivers.
No classroom can have two teachers.
No team can have two captains.
No servant can have two masters.
No broth can have two cooks.

5. Kandathiparambil, *Goodnews Praarthana Gaanamaalika,* 364.

If the Roman soldiers divided Jesus' garments
and cast lots for his clothing,
the followers of Christ divided his church,
which is the body of Christ,
into thirty thousand denominations,
each with its own captains and masters to suit their agenda
at the whims and fancy of every newly hatched member,
forgetting Christ and his cross,
and these actions of some followers of Christ proclaim
that they stand behind neither Christ nor his cross
but whatever suits their agenda.

A couple of years ago Alpha was approached by Beta,
a new immigrant, to help him find a job.
Alpha remembered Delta, his friend,
who had connections with a good pastor
who was well known for finding jobs for others.
Hence Alpha contacted Delta
and requested a job for the jobless Beta.
Delta asked Alpha to wait for two days
and after two days Delta called Alpha
and gave the happy news that the pastor
had agreed to give a job to Beta,
but under one condition:
that Beta should join the pastor's church.
Alpha inquired as to the whereabouts of the church,
and upon hearing Delta's answer, Alpha's eyes rolled.
The answer was:
"The church is new and it is inside the pastor's house.
The current members are the pastor, the pastor's wife,
myself, and two other friends as of now, and
we will become a bigger church sooner than later."
The poor Catholic Beta preferred poverty to apostasy.

The pagan Romans were much better
than many defecting Christians.

Part IV

The former cast lots for Jesus' clothes,
but the latter dismembered Jesus' body itself,
and the dismembering is still going on.
To add fuel to the fire, the various factions
are fighting one another to such an extent that
it is an open secret that many of them do not follow Christ
since common sense, which is not so common,
tells us that people who follow a common goal
try to create union, not division.

Christ did not die for Catholics or Protestants
or for the Lutherans, Methodists, or any other faction.
He is not a tribal, sectarian, or nationalistic god.
Being the unique and universal Savior,
his salvific sacrifice is for the whole world,
and his salvation is also for the anonymous Christians
who follow his path carrying their crosses,
better than some of the baptism-registered Christians,
and this without knowing him or registering under his banner.

Jesus was tempted by the fallen Cherubim twice:
The first before the beginning of his ministry,
when Satan showed him all the sublunary pleasures
of hedonism, materialism, and egoism,
and the second, at the end of his ministry,
with excruciating sufferings and tribulations,
hoping to make him veer away from the will of God.

The golden rule is that if I have no sufferings in the world
I have already lost my battle and am on the broad way to hell
and need to make a strategic U-turn.
If I am swarmed by sufferings and tribulations,
I can rejoice and be glad:
I am on the narrow way, leading to Calvary,
carrying all my crosses that were given to me,
for suffering is the marker of love, and love is God,

and God is love and I have completed my task
of being the image and likeness of God
down here on earth and I can say at the last minute,
"It is consummated."[6]

Grant me the grace to grasp through faith
what my human senses fail to understand about
thy wonderful redemption of the world
irrespective of race, caste, religion, or creed,
and the real meaning of thy cross itself.

What thanks can I offer you, my Lord and my God,
for showing me how to carry the cross
and for redeeming my soul from eternal damnation?
I will laud your name, my Lord and my God,
I will chant and applaud your name forever.

What thanks can I offer you, my Lord and my God,
for creating this wonderful universe,
with everything in it evolving in time,
from mountain ranges to the littlest sparrows,
each with its own role to play on earth,
and to make human life possible on earth,
and for creating me in your own image and likeness

6. John 19:30 (CPDV).

28

God: The Omnipresent Benefactor

Wherever I look or turn around,
everywhere I see your precious gifts.
Wherever I look or turn around,
everywhere I see your omnipresence.

I see you in my wonderful parents.
I see you in my teachers and clergy.
I see you in my brothers and sisters.
I see you in all my family members.
I see you in the needy around me.
I see you in my neighbors and friends.
I see you in all the good Samaritans,
who helped me to survive.
I see myself as your replica,
as I am made in your own image and likeness.

I see you behind nature.
I see you behind the rolling seasons.
I see you behind the alternating days and nights.
I see you behind the rising sun.
I see you behind the waxing crescent.
I see you behind the deep blue sky.
I see you behind the twinkling stars.
I see you behind the shooting stars.

I see you behind the lightning and thunder.
I see you behind the moving clouds.
I see you behind the pouring rains.
I see you behind the falling snow.
I see you behind the aquifers and springs.
I see you behind the gold and diamond mines.
I see you behind the cooling breeze.
I see you behind the passing winds.

I see you behind the food on my table.
I see you behind the fruits and drinks.
I see you behind the fish in the rivers and seas.
I see you behind the birds in the sky.
I see you behind the domestic animals.
I see you behind the wild animals.
I see you behind the ants and roaches.
I see you behind the trees and bushes.
I see you behind the mountains and valleys.
I see you behind the hills and dales.
I see you behind the oceans and lakes.
I see you behind the flowing rivers and rivulets.

I see you behind every motion in the world.
I see you behind every creature in the world.
I see you behind every being in the world.
I see you behind every athlete and artist.
I see you behind every inventor and pioneer.
I see you behind every talented person.
I see you behind every physically challenged person.
I see you behind every mentally challenged person.
I see you behind my blinking eyes.
I see you behind my basic reflexes.
I see you behind my inhalations.
I see you behind my exhalations.
I see you behind my throbbing heart.
I see you behind my beating pulse.
I see you behind my fleeting *nows*.

Part IV

Wherever I look or turn around,
everywhere I see your precious gifts.
Wherever I look or turn around,
everywhere I see your omnipresence.

Forgive my ungratefulness
to such a great benefactor!
Forgive the world's ungratefulness
to such a great benefactor!
Look not at our iniquities,
but look at our concupiscence.
Look not at our failures,
but look at our perseverance and tenacity
akin to that of a toddler learning to walk
getting up from every fall and toddling again.

What thanks can I offer you, my Lord and my God,
for showering me with priceless gifts!
I will open my eyes to see and appreciate your gifts
whenever I turn around and wherever I look.
I will laud your name, my Lord and my God,
I will chant and applaud your name forever.

Endorsements

THE MOST CREATIVE OUTCOME of the COVID-19 pandemic is that people have begun to think about the gifts of human life, nature, and God. When we go through the pages of this beautiful book, *Psalms of COVID-19*, we are filled with a sense of gratitude for all that we have received from God, nature, and others; we begin to appreciate rather than complain; we resort to cherish rather than discard; we begin to protect what we have been given rather than exploit them; and ultimately, we become more generous rather than selfish.

When we identify selfishness as the ground of almost all the issues in the human world, inculcating the sense of gratitude would be the only alternative that can illumine our minds, make us happier, and help us think positively about the gifts we have received. How much less we have appreciated our parents, our family, our body, our senses, our selves! Actually, being thankful towards all of them would positively change our attitudes and ambitions.

COVID-19 has highlighted the importance of mental health in our daily survival. How many people struggle today with loss of hope! For them, too, the best medicine would be to appreciate the gifts they have received all through their lives and for which they need to look back at their lives, look around nature, and to value the precious gifts everywhere. I think Matthew Palai's beautiful book, *Psalms of COVID-19*, would be a good catalyst to help us become more grateful, more positive, and healthier. It's simple, inspiring, and tranquilizing.

✝ *[signature]*

Bishop Thomas Tharayil

EPARCHY OF FARIDABAD
Syro-Malabar Catholic Diocese

Dear Matthew Palai,

I congratulate you for this remarkable work, which is beautifully drafted in the model of the Psalms. The reflections therein suit very much to the contemporary situation beset with the pandemic of COVID-19, which sets forth towards the third wave. These lines sooth the psyche with a healing touch and take the readers to the divine power.

The opening words on gratitude as virtue, duty and justice are quite befitting to the contents of the book. It is explained in simple style substantiating by modest examples and supported by the teachings of the Fathers of the Church. Focusing on the traditional family, the responsible role of the parents is highlighted.

The second part begins with oxygen - the soul of life, which flows into a poem of environmental eulogy on water, earth, trees, atmosphere, sun, wind etc. The mountains and animals do get their share and their place in the universe is duly highlighted. Going through these lines, reminds the reader of the "Laudato si " of St. Francis of Assisi and its subsequent version of the Encyclical of Pope Francis. An interesting section is devoted to staple food and universal food. The author then elucidates how the misuse of these elements leads to ingratitude towards the environment, the other and the Almighty.

The beautiful meditation ends with a Christological trait of the cross of Christ and its salvific mission, followed by an intense prayer.

While felicitating you for this commendable work, I wish a wider readership of this volume "Psalms of COVID-19".

+ Bharakulang-

Archbishop Dr. Kuriakose Bharanikulangara
Diocese of Faridabad

Bishop's House, 18/32 N.E.A., Old Rajindra Nagar, New Delhi 110060, India
E-mail: faridabaddiocese@gmail.com; Tel. (+91)9990326245; (+91)1125759160

Bibliography

Kandathiparambil, Joseph. *Goodnews Praarthana Gaanamaalika.* Kottayam, India: St. Joseph's Orphanage, 2005.

Syromalabar Church. *Syromalabar Sabhayude Qurbana Kramam.* Changanacherry, India: Liturgy Commission, 1989.

Manufactured by Amazon.ca
Bolton, ON